MONEY
SEX
&
Spiritual
Power

MONEY
SEX
&
Spiritual
Power

KEITH DRURY

MONEY SEX & SPIRITUAL POWER
Copyright © 1992 by Wesley Press

Wesley Press
P.O. Box 50434
Indianapolis, Indiana 46250-0434

Library of Congress Cataloging in Publication Data

Drury, Keith W.
      Money Sex & Spiritual Power
Wesley Press: Indianapolis, Ind.: Keith Drury (c) 1992 1. Christian Living
2. Holiness 3. Title
                  ISBN 0-89827-103-7

Printed in the United States of America

CONTENTS

PREFACE ...

I'm a pretty decent hobby carpenter. I especially like to build things with new wood. I like framing the best — there's so much quick progress, and the wood smells so fresh and clean.

What I don't like is renovation work. My wife and I gutted a little "mother-in-law house" in our backyard a few years ago and started over. I didn't like working with that old dusty wood. I'd rather be the first to handle a piece of timber.

For some time now my publisher has been asking me to collect in one book the various thoughts and writings on materialism, sexual temptation, family life, holiness, and spiritual growth. I've resisted the notion. Some of these things have already been circulated in a small booklet or memo format among some pastors and leaders. It's like my woodworking preferences. I don't like working with old stuff. I get tired of the things I wrote about last week, let alone last year. I'd rather sit down and write a whole new book from scratch, where I can drive the first nail.

The publisher prevailed. Apparently there is some demand for reading and study on some of these subjects. So I gutted this old house and renovated each chapter. But, I couldn't help it . . . I wrote a half dozen new chapters . . . just in case you're like me, and mostly like new stuff.

— Keith Drury

PART ONE

MONEY

. . . .

"The subject Jesus taught most
about which we obey the least."

How To Get Rich Slow

T here has seldom been such keen interest in money as there has been these last few years. People pay high prices to attend seminars on how to get rich in real estate or through shrewd investments in stocks. People want to get rich quick.

But only a few will ever get rich in a year or two. Most of us — if we ever do get rich — will get that way slowly, not fast.

If you observe the following tips, the chances are good that you'll wind up rich eventually:

1. Pay God first

Do your giving to God off the top as the first "bill" you pay. Paying God first reminds you that everything is actually under God's control and that you are submitting all your finances to God. God tends to bless those who support His work.[1]

2. Get out of debt, then stay out

Get out of debt quickly, then stay out permanently. Going into debt spends future income for present living. This "have-it-now — pay-for-it-later" mentality is neither good economics nor good Christianity. Debt-free families get a ten to twenty percent discount on life. When you are out of debt, you will be able to spend your income on present needs and wants, not just to pay for past living. Going into consumer debt can even mean you are paying now for things which are already worn-out or broken. It is pure "live-now-pay-later" philosophy, and essentially anti-Christian. As a Christian you should try to get out of consumer debt at least. And, if you are really smart, you'll go on to reduce all debt as quickly as possible.

Pay off installment loans first, then auto loans, then home equity loans, and finally even consider accelerated payments on your mortgage. Once you are completely debt-free, your income will seem huge compared to what you now have left after paying your bills. I recognize that during times of hyper-inflation it seems smart to borrow as much as you can and pay back with "cheap dollars." However, the essential "live-now-pay-later" philosophy is the same. How will you teach your teenagers to "wait" sexually if your family has seldom waited materially? Getting out of debt is smart. And if you're living a "have-it-now-pay-later" life-style, getting out of debt is also the Christian thing to do.

3. Develop frugal habits early

Just because you are poor doesn't mean you're frugal. In fact, poverty sometimes has the opposite effect. We can figure, "Since things are so hopeless, let's live it up tonight." But the chances of developing frugality when you have less are better than after you are rich. So start now. Perhaps you *have* to be frugal just to make ends meet now. Here is a great irony. The seeds of riches lie in poverty, if we respond right. If you are poor, and you learn a lifetime habit of living on less, this simplicity, combined with hard work, will lead to riches. It's much harder for a rich young couple to learn frugality than a poor couple. So, if you have little, thank God for the opportunity to develop a life habit of frugality.

The advantage of learning frugal habits is that they are just that — habits. Even when you no longer "need to scrimp" you still will. Frugality means you live on what you need, not on what you want. Frugality divorces expenses from income and attaches them to needs. The question will be, Do I really need it? not, Can I really afford it? It is obvious what a lifetime effect this habit has. Once you learn the habit, your expenses will not automatically climb each time your income increases. Thus you will begin having more left over with every raise in pay.

Our family learned a variety of frugal habits when we had little to live on. As a result, we purchase food wholesale in bulk — right down to spending several dollars on twenty pounds of salt (which turned out to be a lifetime supply!). We accept lots of hand-me-down clothes (until our kids turn 16!). We drive old cars which we usually sell five years later for more than what we paid for them. But these are our personal habits. There is no one system of frugality for all families. What we do might seem "going too far" to you. And what you choose might seem "radical" to us. Each family must carve out its own frugal practices, and we can't judge each other on our own scale.

A penny saved is not a penny earned. It's more. Saved money is tax-

and interest-free. Besides, there is a spiritual issue here too. Living a simple life on purpose keeps us closer to the basics, and thus removes the "materialistic fog" in our lives which God has such difficulty penetrating.[2]

4. Become a generous person

Give generously, everywhere. Sure, give to the church, but give elsewhere too. Avoid falling into the trap of considering your church-giving your total contribution to God and others. We in the organized church often leave the impression that stewardship and generosity are synonyms for church-giving. We forget to emphasize how Jesus taught a life-style of giving to all, not just to organized religion. Of course, the church needs money. But limiting your giving to the church while you shut off generosity to other individuals will produce a stingy pattern of giving. If you shut up your compassionate heart to a friend at work, even though you are paying your tithe, how can the love of God be in your heart? Christian generosity runs deeper than giving to organizations for tax credit. It includes an overall spirit of giving which starts at church but extends to all people. If you practice this kind of generous life-style, God will bless you with even more to give.

5. Work hard

Hard work and money are connected. Sure, you might get "lucky" sometime and make money without working hard. But basing life on a "lottery mentality," expecting to get rich without hard work, is not Christian. Work hard, give a fair day's work . . . plus a little more, for a fair day's pay. Avoid laziness, which will guarantee poverty. In fact, forget the association between hard work and money all together, and just focus on working hard. Learn to enjoy hard work. Teach your kids to work hard . . . even if they complain at first. Once you develop the habit of always working extra, money will seek you out. *Money gravitates toward work.*

6. Delay major purchases

Many young families practice the philosophy, "If you want it, buy it." As soon as the old washing machine breaks, we rush out to get a new one simply because "the wash is piling up." We wouldn't think of going without a TV for a few months if the old one breaks down. Instead, we frantically rush out the next day to replace it. We don't give God time to work.

Rather than making an immediate purchase, if we would put everything on hold for a couple of weeks, God might save us the price of a new washer. Perhaps He will send a friend your way who will "take a look at it" only to find a simple connection problem which he fixes for free. Or after a couple of visits to the laundromat you'll find someone who says, "Hey, we've got an old washer we're selling for five dollars if you'll haul it away." That washer will last you for five more years. Or your husband (who's never even seen the inside of a washing machine) will take the back off and fiddle with it a while and when he puts it back together it works perfectly (he then pretends he knows how he fixed it!). Or a repairman might fix it for far less than you could get a new one. Or maybe the washing machine just fixes itself and mysteriously starts working again in a few weeks!   These things happen! We've seen each of them in our twenty-five years of marriage. But it takes time. The point is, waiting a while may eliminate the need to buy something new.

Delaying major purchases also gives God time to work in your own mind. What you now feel is an absolute necessity may not seem so important after a three-week "cooling off" period. Sometimes God does not provide the wanted item. Instead He changes your desire to have it. Either way, He fully provides your needs (Philippians 4:19).

7. Start saving

Saving is not the initial smart financial step. The first step is getting out of debt. Once you quit "having it now; paying for it later," you can take the second step: "Having it now; paying for it now" — living off your current income. Only when you get out of debt and are living on what you make, should you move to the third step: "Paying for it now; having it later." This third step of delayed gratification is probably where we all should have started out! But most of us come to it slowly, and thus get rich much later in life than those who practice this discipline from the beginning. "Third step saving" practices let you enjoy the anticipation of having something in the future, while you save up for it. Looking forward to the purchase is sometimes as much fun as having the thing itself. And there is a side benefit. Sometimes after saving up for so long, you understand the real cost and it is impossible for you to shell out the cash to buy it. How many of us really would plunk down $20,000 cash for a new car? Cash? If we all bought cars with saved-up cash, Detroit would become a ghost town! But don't worry, most people won't even read this book. And most of the people who do read it will ignore this advice anyway, so there'll still be plenty of jobs for your Michigan friends.

How to save? Initially start saving up for major purchases — a TV, major appliances, big vacation, second car, and finally maybe even your family car. Some even say you should save up for a house, but this certainly cannot apply to everyone. The idea here is to start saving something. Like church-giving, it is a statement you are making which flows against the "have-it-now-pay-later" philosophy of life.

8. Keep money secondary

Seeking wealth is self-defeating. The more you chase it, the more you'll get, but the less satisfied you'll be. There will always be somebody richer than you. If you want to get rich — either quick or slow — you are on a slippery slope. Instead, seek to serve others, to work hard, to seek God's kingdom first . . . and money will get added as you travel along (Matthew 6:33). Money is a by-product of service and work. For the Christian, money is a "sideline," never the "bottom line" (Luke 12:15).

9. Make long-haul decisions

Sometimes spending more money *now* will save you money later. A good pair of shoe trees might cost more now, but will give you an extra few years of life on your shoes. When we built our home, we added additional insulation and geo-thermal heat. These long-haul investments cost more at first, but will pay back dividends increasingly as long as we live in the house (and to our successors, *and* the environment). These kinds of expenses are really long-term investments.

Most of us live so much for the present that we seldom have the cash to make long-haul decisions. This is how "the rich get richer; the poor get poorer." It is a deadly cycle. Not investing the cash to make long-haul decisions now simply ensures we won't have the cash later to make other long-haul decisions.

10. Borrow and loan things

Being the independent folk we are, most of us hate to borrow or rent something. Our own self-reliance demands we "get one for myself." True, sometimes it is better to purchase an item — if over the years it will "pay for itself." But often we simply want to have it now. However, in figuring this out we need to be careful. I hate renting things, so I can always crunch the figures enough to prove I can justify buying something for myself. I don't like borrowing either. It seems so humiliating, almost unbiblical, doesn't it? Many of us figure the proverb, "Neither a borrower nor a lender be" is somewhere in the Bible. But you'll find it in Shakespeare's *Hamlet*, Act I, scene 3, not the Bible.

But borrowing and loaning make good sense, especially for Christians. After all, early Christians did not consider anything they had as their own and shared everything with each other.[3] And Jesus instructed us never to turn away those who would borrow from us (Matthew 5:42).

As for Jesus, consider His life: He was born in a borrowed stable, raised by a borrowed dad, got several key disciples He borrowed from John the Baptist, taught from a borrowed boat, slept on borrowed mats, multiplied a borrowed lunch, rode into Jerusalem on a borrowed donkey, held the Last Supper in a borrowed room, and was buried in a borrowed tomb.

Of course, we shouldn't be irresponsible moochers.[4]   But borrowing saves you money over the long haul, and lending saves others money. When Christians borrow and lend, it releases more money for the kingdom of God, eliminating duplicate expenses all over town for items which could be loaned to each other.

11. Teach your kids about money

If your children are still at home, start early teaching these principles. Give them an allowance as soon as they have felt material needs (the day they reach out grasping for something at the store). Remind them to take along their money when you go to the store. Let each choose how to spend it, even on foolish purchases. It is better for them to learn on a lost dollar now than learn on lost thousands later.

As they grow older, help them earn money beyond your parental "welfare payments." Teach them the connection between hard work and money. Let them learn the principles of giving, blessing, and saving by practicing them. Though you should remind them from time to time, don't protect them from failures. If they squander all their money on some frivolous purchase and wind up broke the day of the deposit for their school's ski trip, don't bail them out. Such pain will be a lifetime lesson. (Actually this lesson is better taught when the child is a preschooler with a small allowance — the more principles they learn before age eight, the better!)

By the time your children are teenagers, you might be able to teach them business principles as well — (1) Capital formation — saving or borrowing money; (2) Investing capital — purchasing equipment or products with which to make money; (3) Labor — working with the equipment or products; (4) Value-adding — making the product or service of greater value by applying labor; (5) Mark-up — selling for more than you paid for it; (6) Profit — the net dollars "clear" made on the product or service. These lessons will carry your children through their lifetime if you take time to teach them now.

My oldest son, David, started learning these principles in seventh grade by purchasing a cassette tape duplicating machine. He began copying tapes for churches, a college, and various traveling speakers. He was able to make enough to save up enough cash to buy a second machine. He continued to duplicate tapes, sometimes himself, sometimes hiring friends to work for him. By his junior year of high school, he had made and saved enough money for a down payment on a house in the town where he intended to go to college. He sold the tape business, purchased the home and has rented it out with a positive cash flow ever since. The income will help him through the rest of his college years.

In seventh grade, my youngest son, John, bought a trailer load of landscaping mulch which he packaged in large bags to sell door to door for cash income. (We had moved to the country, so he had space to store it!) Besides this immediate cash flow project, we are helping him plant a thousand tiny trees every spring break in the field behind our house. He intends to sell them in 6-10 years to pay for his college.

These are just one family's ideas. To some, these ideas sound impractical if not impossible. The point is that every family has some way their daughters and sons *could* make money. Just look around you. There are jobs for teenagers at fast food establishments and shopping malls. There are babysitting needs near you. There are even businesses they could run themselves with a little encouragement from a parent or grandparent. Whatever you do, your kids can learn that money is related to creativity and hard work.

12. Let God bless you

Really! He can and will do it. God doesn't need your money — you need His! If you really believe He owns it all, then He can bless you with some of it if He wants to.[5] Can He trust you? Are you a good investment? Will you simply waste it all on yourself? Or will the things closest to His heart get your support? What evidence does God have that you are so faithful in handling what He's already given you, He should bless you with more? (Matthew 25:21, 23)

It is my observation that God usually blesses people who "can handle it." If you follow the above principles for years, the natural results are that you will become rich. The principles and practices themselves produce wealth. But beyond that, God sometimes chooses to bless His good stewards with "bonus" blessings! These are undeserved extras He pours on top of those produced by hard work, saving, and frugality.

Perhaps you'll sell your home after a dozen years or so for twice what you paid for it. Maybe a friend will invite you to join him in a land purchase and you'll make thousands of dollars in a single year. Or you might give three weeks of your time to do a project for free — never expecting anything out of it — then, ten years later it brings you thousands of dollars. You may be praying about funds to replace your roof when a hailstorm damages it so much that your insurance company will completely replace it at no cost to you. You might somehow get free use of a brand-new car. Or, perhaps a little boy you taught years ago in your church will grow up and offer to build a house for you at an unbelievable bargain. Are these things mere coincidences? Could God bless you this way? He can. These things happen. I know . . . in the last five years each happened to me. Make God's kingdom first priority and who knows what He'll add to you! (Matthew 6:33)

13. Then . . . beware!

When you've followed all of the tips above, and you've kept them up for many years, you will likely wind up rich. That is, you will have no debt, some savings, simple needs, and your income will be more than you spend. That is *rich*. You are rich when you have more than you need.

But, then you will face a new problem. *It will be harder for you to get to heaven.* Not impossible, mind you . . . just harder. You will tend to trust in your savings instead of God. You may become proud and take personal credit for being so well off, thinking that you are smarter than everybody else. And it will be harder, not easier, to give. For instance, after being so frugal for many years, you'll have a hard time giving to anyone or any organization who seems to waste your gift by living higher than you do. You may get more selfish as a rich person than you ever were when you were poor. Your possessions will dull your spiritual fervor, and "the good life" will take the edge off your concern for the lost.

If you do wind up with more income than you need, it could poison your own soul. In fact, if you continually pile up more riches on earth, you will gradually absorb a toxic level of materialism into your soul. You could go to hell rich. What good would it be to gain the whole world and lose your own soul?

So what should you do if you become rich? There is only one antidote to the poison of wealth: *giving*. This is the only way to keep riches from destroying your own soul. It is the only way to be rich in the afterlife. You must habitually and freely give — pass your money through to God's work and others. If you can happily maintain the habit of unselfish giving, you might still get into heaven . . . even if you are rich. After all, it's not *impossible* for a rich person to be saved — it's just *harder*.[6]

Endnotes:

1. *God tends to bless those who support His work.* While God's blessings are related to our giving, getting more should not be our motive for giving to God's work. If our motive is giving-to-get we are not giving generously but selfishly, and God loves (and blesses) a generous giver, not a selfish one.

2. By *frugality* here I do not mean being cheap (buying everything so cheap that it self-destructs and turns out being a poor investment). Neither do I intend to suggest that Christians shouldn't buy an expensive gift at times. Once in a while we should "break the alabaster box" and give lavishly. It is possible to become just as materialistic in frugality as in spending. But it's far less common. For most of us, the problem is being too lavish on ourselves, not on others.

3. The *earliest believers* treated everything as common property though held in trust by the individual for the common good. As one of the Christians had a need, another would sell something to meet that need (Acts 2:44-45). Further explanation of this Christian practice of sharing occurs two chapters later where we are told, "No one claimed that any of his possessions was his own, but they shared everything they had" (Acts 4:32). Most of us today treat this practice of early Christians as an aberration rather than the norm. However, this kind of free giving, sharing, loaning and borrowing should be normal for a Spirit-filled Christian community.

4. *...irresponsible moocher.* I am not recommending "living off the land" by borrowing everything from others and abusing the privilege. Along with borrowing goes the analogous responsibility to return the item — cleaner, improved, filled up, or fixed up. And of course, *remember* to return it! And make sure it's a two-way street — that you lend as well as borrow. That means you should buy some things to loan to others and tell them you've got it, and are willing to loan it out.

5. *Let God bless you.* We must be careful to avoid confusing God's blessing with the false "prosperity gospel." God can and does bless His children but not always materially. To expect riches as a rightful inheritance because we are His children is presumption. Remember, He gave His Son a cross. Nevertheless, God does often bless His children with more than they need... sometimes even pressed down, and overflowing! If we will be patient and give Him time to work through others, He sometimes will bless us with far more than we need. This is the blessing addressed here. Such blessing is not a reward, but a tool — for us to use as a steward.

6. John Wesley instructed his followers to "*Get* all you can" and "*Save* all you can." But then he added a *third* directive: "*Give* all you can." When Mr. Wesley died at the ripe old age of 88, he left behind only his dying testimony ("Best of all, God is with us"), two or three personal items of relatively inconsequential value, *and* the Methodist movement!

CHAPTER 2

THE MOST ACCEPTED SIN IN THE CHURCH

A t coffee break one morning, I heard about a prayer meeting where the people were asked to quote their favorite verse. One fellow in that prayer meeting piped up with, "I don't remember where it's found, but I like the one that goes, 'Treat yourself to the best.'"

He failed to quote the rest of the "verse". . ."Treat yourself to the best . . . chew Mail Pouch Tobacco." He'd read it on the side of a barn, not in the Book of Books. Too many Christians are getting their theology "off the side of the barn" instead of from God's Book. The Book says, "Deny yourself, take up your cross, and follow me." The barn says, "I take care of myself," "I'm worth it," "I can afford it," or "I deserve it." The barn produces books like *How to Get What You Want, Winning Through Intimidation, Looking Out For Number One, Pulling All the Strings.* But the Book stands firm . . . and says, "If any man would be my disciple, let him deny himself, take up his cross, and follow me."

We live in a culture which tells us it is okay to crave more . . . this is the "American way." The dominant value of our culture is, What will I get out of it? or What's in it for me? We are being told that true meaning in life will come through the acquisition of more things. Our income must rise each year. Our net worth should go up. Television delivers a nightly diet of hard-core "materialistic pornography" . . . blatantly promoting lust for possessions.

It is a lie. The Book describes the true believer as one who is able to swim upstream against his or her culture . . . especially in this matter of money and possessions.

In the book *Disciple*, Juan Carlos Ortiz says we have invented the fifth gospel. We know of the Gospel according to Matthew, Mark, Luke, and John. But we've invented a fifth gospel . . . the "Gospel according to St.

Evangelical." Ortiz writes, "We take all the verses we like — all those offering something, promising a benefit, focusing on what we get — and we make a systematic theology of these verses." The result? We wind up with the theology of the money changers — the gospel of the big offer, the gospel of the hot sale. We like this gospel of Aladdin's Lamp . . . we think we can rub the Lord with a little bit of prayer and get anything we want.

Sure, we should be concerned about secular humanism or New Age teachings in our schools. But we should be more concerned about *secular materialism* in the church. Whole movements are springing up based on this "fifth gospel." We are being taught that if our faith is strong enough, we can have *anything* we want from God. "Prosperity gospel" hucksters teach us that as children of the King of Kings, we should *expect* to be prosperous. And some of the evangelical movement have adopted this theology, or at least part of it. It sounds good to us. It soothes our consciences. It's clever to make God the cosmic bellhop in the sky. Like the medieval people who thought the earth was the center of the universe, we have come to act as if *man* is the center of the universe, and God and Jesus Christ and all the angels revolve around *us* just waiting to relieve our latest headache, get us a lucrative job, find us a convenient parking space, or help us get our locker door open.

We are wrong. The Book is right: God is at the center of all. And He has more important things to do than make your and my life more convenient. He says, "If any man would be my disciple, let him deny himself, take up his cross, and follow me."

Naturally, this "prosperity gospel" appeals to many. People like to be told, "God wants you to prosper." It is a special problem in North America where we pragmatists sanctify *anything that works.* This teaching seems to bring many into the kingdom of God . . . or at least into the organized church.

One does not need to travel far to see that we are pretty impressed with the fifth gospel. Evangelicals have become a church of the middle class, maybe even upper middle class in some places. Our church buildings are no longer located "across the railroad tracks." Our members dress well and live in tidy suburban homes. They drive carefully maintained recent-model cars . . . maybe even two or three cars. We can look at and congratulate ourselves on our remarkable upward mobility — "We've come a long way, Baby."

But are we in danger of becoming just another middle-class group which sanctifies the cultural values and waters down Christ's call to radical discipleship? Have we become too impressed with wealth and power? Have we adopted the culture's dominant value of "What will I get out of it?" or "What's in it for me?"

And let's quit kidding ourselves . . . we even *tithe to ourselves* as Tom Sine rudely reminds us in his *Mustard Seed Conspiracy*. We plead for people to give offerings to God; then we spend it so that we may have softer pews, nicer carpeting, excellent handball courts, and better air conditioning.[1] Does God need these things? I know of one church where they passed a rule and hung up a sign stating "no outsiders may use this church gym." No wonder there is a movement to tax churches — many of us have become little more than ingrown social clubs organized for our own benefit. Some churches have even figured out how to make missions offerings benefit themselves. They simply dip into the missions offerings for their own expenses for "local missions" including bus ministries or VBS or even to finance the pastor and board's missionary tour expenses. It is not uncommon for a local church's "missions budget" to have as much as 25 percent of the money actually never leave the local church![2]

Is it any wonder the world doesn't take us seriously? We are caught up in the same rat race as they are. The rats are winning! We desperately grasp to better ourselves materially, while at the same time we mouth spiritual platitudes like "Only one life, 'twill soon be past, only what's done for Christ will last." This is secular materialism at its worst. It doesn't matter what we *say* because our ploys speak far louder than our platitudes! Our motives drown out our mottos! Materialism is *living* as if the material matters most.

Into the midst of our secular materialism marches the radical Jesus with His command, "If anyone would come after me, he must deny himself, take up his cross, and follow me." We have accepted the cushy concepts, "*Take care of* yourself," "*Love* yourself," "*Be* yourself," and "*Find* yourself." Jesus says, "*Deny* yourself."

There is precious little self-denial among us today. I dislike self-denial. Do you? Take fasting, for instance. We call it "fasting" when we go without a meal. We can't bring ourselves to deny our physical longings for food for even a few days or a week for the sake of our spiritual welfare or for lost souls.

But the denial Jesus calls for is deeper than going without one meal a week or giving up ice cream for Lent. In fact, it is more than self-denial. It is *denial of self*. Christ is saying, "If you want to follow me, you'll have to make a deliberate choice to put God first, others second, and you must get at the end of the line."

We don't like being at the end of the line. The world says, Put yourself first, others second, and if you have a little room at the end, make a nice little place for Jesus. God says the opposite.

Is it any wonder that most churches have not experienced a spiritual revival? It is Jesus who said, "If you have not been trustworthy in handling worldly wealth, who will trust you with true riches?" (Luke 16:11). Can't we recognize the fact that if we are not faithful in handling our money and possessions, God will not grant us true riches — spiritual riches? *The use of our money is the best single indicator of our level of commitment.* And for most of us, that means we fail miserably, for we spend most of our money on ourselves, and at best, give God a "ten percent cut."

Jesus calls us to a different and *radical* life-style. Jesus has called us to abandon the world's materialistic life-style — an endless quest for more. He calls us to adopt a new approach to living — denial of self for the sake of the unfinished task of declaring the gospel worldwide, and caring for those who are needy.

But *why*? Why should you live on less than you earn? Why should you pass up that second car for the sake of a missionary's salary? Why should you get rid of that comfortable stack of possessions for the sake of extending the kingdom of Christ? There are at least four reasons:

1. God commands it

God said, "Do not steal," and "Do not commit adultery." But it was the same God who said, "Do not pile up treasures on earth." Who gave us the right to decide which of God's commandments are compulsory and which are optional? "Pile up" simply means just that — to constantly add more to what we already have. How many of us are guilty of a life-style of adding more possessions to what we've already got?

I am. I remember that tiny trailer we used for our first move. Everything we owned fit neatly in a 4 X 6 foot space. Look at us now! The last time we moved we had a whole moving van load. Little by little my family has "piled up" things we needed or thought we did. Sure, I can look around and compare my possessions with some others and figure I'm no worse than the next guy. But that does not change the fact that I've piled up a bunch of possessions over the first twenty-five years of marriage. Piling up treasures on earth is wrong because Jesus said don't do it. Purposefully piling up more stuff is willful disobedience to God's commandment (Matthew 6:19-20). This is one reason why we Christians need to swim upstream in our materialistic culture. If you're like me, you've got more than you ever had. We need to confess that such piling up is wrong and it needs to be reversed if we are to stay in obedience to Christ.

2. Materialism is a serious sin

Greed — living a life largely dedicated to accumulation — is repeatedly listed with all kinds of "serious" sins in the Scriptures. Greed keeps company with immorality, impurity, adultery, homosexuality, thievery, and the like (Ephesians 5:5; 1 Corinthians 6:9; Colossians 3:5-6). We even remove people from church membership for adultery, homosexual practices, or stealing. When was the last time you heard of anyone being kicked out of the church for being greedy? We accept greed as one of the "better" sins . . . even respectable. So we "sanctify" greed. Until we come to consider the sin of greed as just as serious as adultery, we'll never overcome this one.

3. Materialism is a mirage

Everything you and I have piled up will all melt anyway. "The heavens will disappear with a roar, the elements will be destroyed by fire." That shiny new car, newly painted house, brand-new dishwasher, powerful motorcycle, attractive summer cottage, efficient riding lawn mower, stamp collection, even that electric garage door opener — IT ALL WILL MELT! And since everything is going to be destroyed, how then ought we to live? (2 Peter 3:10-11).

Following a certain rich man's death, a nosy guest asked the dead man's friend, "How much did he leave behind?" The friend answered, "Everything."

How true. If the Lord comes, it all melts, and if you die first, it "all goes back into the box" like the end of a Monopoly game. You can't take it with you.

The quest for material possessions is an empty well. It is a drink that never satisfies. If you ask the man earning $25,000 a year how much it would take to satisfy him, he will say $30,000. The man earning $50,000 will say $100,000. The man earning $100,000 will say $250,000. On and on the quest goes — for a life built on the acquisition of material wealth is never satisfied. It is like drinking salt water. The more you drink, the more thirsty you get. Materialism is a mirage — it promises satisfaction it does not and cannot deliver.

4. I deny myself so that I may give

But the highest motivation for adopting a life-style of self-denial is for the sake of giving. What an exciting motivation for going back to work next Monday! "Doing something useful . . . [so] that [we'll] have something to share with those in need" (Ephesians 4:28). This is "giving living." Earning money so that I have something to share with people in need, and to extend the gospel. This is the greatest reason for a simpler life-style.

John Wesley had a simple three-point sermon on this subject of money. His first point: *Earn all you can.* This is an argument for being industrious. Christians should be hard-working people and not lazy. The second point: *Save all you can.* This is an argument for frugality, not for piling up a huge savings accounts. He was saying as you buy groceries, housing, clothing, and other necessities, "save all you can." Be careful, be frugal in your spending. His third point was the reason for doing the first two: *Give all you can.* This is the foundation of a Christian approach to money — developing a life-style of "giving living." Earning as much as I can, watching my expenses in order to save all I can, so that I will be able to give all I can. Giving is the antidote to materialism's poison.

So what can I do? Is it good enough for me just to feel a little twinge of guilt while I continue the acquisition of more possessions? Should I simply be just a bit more embarrassed about that new car, new tool kit, or new summer cottage? No, guilt will not suffice. God wants obedience in this matter, not just confession. So, what can we do? Are there practical steps you and I can actually take?

Yes, consider the following steps you could take in order to bring your life into line with God's commandment on materialism:

Step 1: Begin unpiling

At least you could do this much to obey Christ's teachings. Simply get rid of some of the stuff you've been piling up. How did you get it all? You simply added a little bit at a time. You now have more than you ever dreamed of. At least you can turn that process around and begin unpiling — even a little bit at a time.

How? Simply reverse the piling up process. When someone comes to your house and admires a lamp — give it to them! If you've got two sets of wrenches, find some young man who has none and give him a set. If you haven't been playing that piano in the front room, find someone who needs it and give it to them. This is the simplest level of response to God's truth. Just reverse your life-style of accumulation by unloading the stuff you've piled up.

When I was in my early thirties, my family started having regular garage sales. We would range through the house and examine every possession we owned — every shirt, every suit, every piece of furniture, every toy, even every tool — and decide if we really needed to keep it another year. It is amazing the pile of possessions we would collect for our sale. Why not hold a garage sale and dedicate the total proceeds to some worthy project? It's a start. There is not a person reading this chapter who could not at least adopt this policy of initial obedience to Christ's command against piling up treasure on earth. Begin unpiling as soon as possible!

Step 2: Sell something big and give away the proceeds

Could it be that one of the reasons the New Testament Church was so dynamic is that from time to time people sold a piece of property or other possession and gave the total proceeds to the church for the distribution to the needy?

This wasn't communism — it was commitment. There was such a spirit of sharing that nobody even considered anything they owned as their own — "Sure, you can borrow anything of mine you want." And it didn't happen constantly — just "from time to time." Maybe that's what you need to do with that summer cottage. How about that boat you seldom use? Is there a power saw you haven't used for years? Are you storing furniture for some unknown reason? Maybe you could sell it and dedicate the total amount received in payment to the Lord.

Just think of the joy you'd get out of giving stuff like this away. Do you have any "big ticket" items you could sell or give to the Lord? Sort of like a "sacrifice" to Him? Is this something you could do? Would it please God?

Step 3: Freeze your keeping

This step is more radical. Could you live on the same amount you earned this year? How about giving yourself a wage freeze? How about making this covenant with the Lord: "Everything above what I earned this year I will pass straight through to You." I call this "Faith-promise living." If you make this commitment to the Lord, watch out! When He knows His work gets 100 percent of the blessings He rains down on you, He often opens the windows of heaven and showers it down! After all, based on the old tithing concept, for God's concerns to get $100, He had to bless you with $1000. Under the "faith-promise living" concept, if God blesses you with an extra $100, His work gets it all!

My family tried this one year and we were shocked to discover the same amount stretched to easily cover expenses, plus God seemed to pass through far more to give to others. We were so encouraged by our dis-covery that we were then able to take a further radical step — *reducing our keeping.*

Step 4: Reduce your keeping

We get this giving thing all mixed up. We talk about *giving,* but God judges us on our *keeping.* The question is not "What do you give?" True stewardship says all money which passes through my hand is God's; therefore, I will keep as little as possible — just what I need. When we praise a rich person's large gift, we assume that God is impressed by the largeness of the gift. But God compares what he gave with what he *kept.* This is the message of Jesus' teaching in response to the "widow's mite" incident. So the question is, "Could you live on less next year than you lived on this year?" What if your salary was cut by $500 next year? $1,000? Could you still make it?

Why not cut it yourself? How about committing yourself to living on less next year than this year — giving all the excess to God's work and needy people? Could you try this? Maybe even for one year? My family practiced keeping less each year for five years in a row and we were absolutely amazed at how much *less* income would stretch *more* each year. We knew we couldn't do this forever. But we tried it a year at a time. At least it was something to do which represented swimming upstream against our materialistic culture. Sure, eventually our tots became teens and we had to give ourselves some raises. But those first five years taught us the joy of living on less. They became a benchmark of antimaterialistic living to which we both intend to return.

I'm not talking about an exercise in self-flagellation as if there is some-thing holy about "doing without." The purpose of living on less is not denial alone — it is giving in order to carry out God's work of extending the gospel and caring for the needy.

Step 5: Sell all, give it away, and follow Jesus somewhere else

We have dodged Christ's command to the rich young ruler in Luke 18 by saying it was instruction to one man in one situation at one time. But what will we do with the identical command given in Luke 12 to the entire flock of Christ's followers? Isn't it possible, just maybe, that God is calling some Christians somewhere today to divest themselves completely of everything in order to follow Him into His work? I admit that this is not Christ's call to everyone, but shouldn't we see this happen once in awhile? When was the last time you heard of someone "selling out" everything and giving all the proceeds away before they went to the mission field or entered the Lord's work? Maybe selling all and putting it in the bank for retirement, but squandering it on the poor? Not likely! I know a few stories and they are inspiring. But if Christ actually is calling some of us to do this, most of us are joining the ruler in walking away sorrowfully. It just seems like too much to ask. *Is it?*

Now, what about you?

Is creeping materialism getting a grip on you? Are you being helplessly towed downstream in our materialistic culture? Is the command of Jesus clear to you? Then, what single step could you take to begin swimming against the current of our culture? Is there at least a tiny beginning step you could take? Why not start today? Now? What could you do to begin?

ENDNOTES:

1. *Does God need these things?* Obviously not. However they can be used for God's work. The point here is not that these things are wrong, but that they can be selfish. It is to remind us that even our giving can be beneficial to ourselves. Little giving is of the "beyond-ourselves-nothing-in-return" calibre.

2. *Selfish missions giving.* While the practice of diverting missions money into locally beneficial needs is increasingly common and accepted, it is sometimes dishonest and perhaps even illegal unless each giver knows exactly where it's going. A "world outreach offering" raised right after a passionate appeal from a foreign missionary may suggest to the giver that the money is going to foreign missions. Unless the giver has been given clear information about where the money is going, such offerings are at least dishonest, and at worst, illegal. If a giver knows part of the money is going to buy a photocopy machine for the church office "to copy missionary letters" at least it is honest.

This is not to say that foreign missions is itself not selfish at times. Some missions organizations use the money they receive primarily for their own staff's benefit with little soul-saving results. But this is no excuse for a local church to use the romance of "world evangelism" to raise more money for their own needs. This approach will simply teach people to figure out ways to "tithe to themselves" personally, like the one ministerial student I heard of who tithed to a fellow ministerial student — using his tithe to "support someone preparing for the ministry." The other student reciprocated and "tithed" his income back to the first student — what a handy way to tithe to yourself! Churches should be above these kinds of shenanigans. (So should ministerial students!)

CHAPTER 3

TRAVELING LIGHT

Sharon Drury

We learned a life-changing lesson about money while hiking the Appalachian Trail for three months as a young couple. It was only one week after we were married that my husband began talking about the two of us going on a great trek across the famed Appalachian Trail in the eastern United States. It had been his life-long goal. The dream eventually infected me too. But the timing wasn't right. We had schooling to complete, bills to pay, and life to get on with.

Then our chance came. My husband had finished seminary, and we seemed to be in an "interim" year. The old dream of trekking on the Appalachian Trail was resurrected. Soon we were in our parents' basement amidst a myriad of backpacking paraphernalia sorting out what to take and what to leave behind. Moccasins to lounge around in after a day in stiff hiking boots would be so comfortable — I packed them in. A tiny transistor radio to keep in touch with the outside world, especially for weather reports — in it went. A small bag of essentials that formed my basic make-up kit — definitely. I was intent on making my three-month journey in the woods as comfortable as possible.

One by one, we carefully packed each item. Satisfied that we had everything we needed, I shouldered my pack and weighed in. Subtracting my own weight, I found my pack weighed about 40 pounds. My husband's pack weighed in at almost 50 pounds. Neither of these were extraordinarily heavy according to the prevailing wisdom of our backpacking friends. We lifted them to our backs, tightened the waist strap snugly, and walked around a bit. They actually felt fairly comfortable — at least in the basement where we'd packed them.

Carrying them on the trail was quite another matter! We started our three-month trek the next day at Springer Mountain, Georgia, where the Appalachian Trail begins (or ends, if you are traveling south). It was a foggy, cold March morning when we saw our first white-painted trail markings that would lead us north toward our goal. Our spirits were high as we signed the hikers' register, proudly listing our destination as the Susquehanna River, 1,000 miles to the north. Tears welled up in my husband's eyes as his life-long dream came to reality.

The pain for the gain

The euphoria quickly wore off. Most of the Appalachian Trail is uphill. I suppose there were downhill sections, but I can't remember any! We trudged along each day from dawn until dusk. At the lean-tos, where we spent each night, we collapsed into our sleeping bags, sometimes too exhausted to fix supper. Through several snowfalls we plodded along with icy feet. We thought, "How could things get worse?"

Then the spring rains came. Our clothes, socks, and shoes stayed soaked for days on end as we slogged northward to our goal. Each day would begin with our crawling out of damp sleeping bags and pulling on cold, soaked clothes which had not dried out one bit overnight.

And our backs ached under the burden of our heavy packs. All we looked forward to was our next hourly rest stop. We began expanding these planned ten-minute stops to 30, 40 minutes . . . eventually to an hour. We dreaded heaving those heavy packs on our backs again. We soon lost all interest in taking the side trails to the many panoramic views along the Appalachian Mountain Range. Yet we plodded on for some strange reason.

I remember one time during this period when my husband, who was leaning forward under his towering load, asked, "Why in the world are we doing this?" I too was bent over looking at the path beneath me. I cynically replied through clenched teeth, "Why, dear, it's to see the scenery!"

The secret discovered

Then we learned the secret of joyful backpacking: *The lighter the load, the greater the joy.* How ironic. The very things we had packed to make our journey comfortable had become the burdens which drained our joy away. I remember the crisp evening when the whole thing caved in on us. We began seeing all the possessions we were toting as enemies — not friends — of our comfort. That very evening, we spread out every single item in our packs and decided which were truly essential in light of their weight.

The results were shocking. All at once my little radio didn't seem nec-

essary any more.   Sure, it was handy, but hearing the reports didn't
change anything — it still rained the next day just the same.   Out went the
radio.   My lounging moccasins, which had seemed so important when I
packed them several weeks before, went in the "luxuries pile" along with
the radio.   My husband's fancy little Swiss knife with a dozen blades and
gadgets to do just about anything you could imagine — well, you can
guess where that went.   My small make-up kit that I had included to maintain my self-dignity in the woods — well, I kept that.   Some things are
clearly necessities!

We had quite a bonfire that night.   Our luxuries — formerly necessities
— went up in smoke.   The items which wouldn't burn were packed in a
special place to give away later.   (There were several Boy Scouts who
eagerly accepted our gifts, never recognizing they then had to carry them
out!)   A few days later, we walked out to a post office and sent home a
whole bag of nonessentials.

What a difference!   We could now swing our packs onto our shoulders
from a standing position instead of sliding into our burdens sitting down,
then staggering to our feet.   No longer were we bent over under enormous
loads.   We began keeping a list of the new birds we were seeing — for the
first time.   At almost every side trail, we would quickly scamper down to
drink in the delicious views of the Appalachian valleys below.

Cutting our weight became a regular diversion for us.   We carefully
compared the weight of every food item we purchased each week.   We
began discarding all the paper wrappings, boxes, and unnecessary por-
tions of food products.   We got rid of our little stove and began cooking
on an open fire.   We even burned the day's section of our guidebook each
night to save the weight of two or three pages!

The more we did without, the more we realized we could do without.
When we crossed the Susquehanna River three months later, I was carrying only twelve pounds, and Keith carried an eighteen-pound pack.   We
had discovered the joy of backpacking — traveling light.   While the
Appalachian Trail experience provided a vast treasury of memories and
gave our marriage a special common bond, it also taught us a lesson
about possessions.

Settling down

Then we settled down.   My husband got an assignment working with
our denominational headquarters, and within a month of completing our
trek on the Appalachian Trail we had moved to Indiana.   We rented a
house, retired our packs to the attic, and began settling into a new routine.

• •

The needs of a normal life were far more sophisticated than trail life. Take clothing for instance. On the trail, I had reduced my needs to one change. Now, as a secretary in an academic community, it seemed I needed seven or maybe even ten outfits as a minimum requirement. Soon my closet began overflowing, and extra outfits had to be stored in the hall closet. We kept the hand-me-down furniture for the family room when we bought new living room furniture. Then, of course, there was the kitchen to outfit with a mixer, toaster oven, dishwasher, blender, food processor, everyday dishes, and special china. All of these seemed like "basic essentials." And, after ten years, we got an electric garage door opener which seemed so essential!

We eventually bought a house, a bit bigger than the one we had rented — after all, we had a child to care for now. Later, we moved to Indianapolis and built our own house — larger still, since we have two teens and my mother-in-law with us now.

Little by little, we accumulated the ingredients of a comfortable life. Sure, we both work hard and take care of our things, but was this really what God wanted for me? Would I ever be done fixing up my house? Was I really happier than ever before? Several Christian speakers addressed the issue of materialism. I cringed. For awhile, at least.

What finally hit me was God's Word itself. Jesus had simply addressed the issue with, "Do not pile up treasures on earth." I had read the verse before, but I'd always been pretty clever in interpreting it to fit my own life-style. I twisted it to mean, "Do not pile up a big pile of treasures on earth," satisfied that my pile was smaller than some of my friends' piles. Or I had read it, "*As* you pile up treasures on earth, do not become attached to them," priding myself in holding things lightly, having committed them all to the Lord. But the Word kept coming back in the simplicity of a clear command: "Do not pile up treasures on earth."

One of the ways I have always been able to tell God is speaking to me is that I keep seeing or hearing a truth everywhere. Here it was in a book I had borrowed. Now again it jumped out from a message by a visiting speaker. Then it surfaced in a magazine article. But most of all, verses kept popping out of the Scriptures: "If we have food and clothing, let us be content" (1 Timothy 6:8). "Contentment also includes my garage door opener, doesn't it, Lord?" "Be on your guard against all kinds of greed" (Luke 12:15). "Who? Me, Lord? Greedy?" "Put to death . . . sexual immorality, impurity, lust, even desires, and greed, which is idolatry." "Lord, why put an innocent thing like greed in with those really serious sins?"

God's Word kept hammering away at me

Then the truth came back to me again. The Lord took me back to my Appalachian Trail experience. He seemed to say, "The truth is the same — the greatest joy comes to those who travel light." A light went on in my head. I kept falling into the same trap again. I was assuming that all these things would produce a more comfortable trip — yet they were loading me down and draining the joy of traveling through this earth. Even when we had accumulated a houseful of nice things, they didn't seem to satisfy — we still "needed" more.

Now the real work began. What were really necessities? What things could we sensibly get rid of? What things were legitimate aids in our ministry to others? How much should we subject our children to? What should we keep until the kids are gone? What do we need to care for my mother-in-law? What is an investment and what is an expense? How far should we go?

None of these answers come easily. We continue to struggle with most of them, sometimes every day. But it's the painful struggle that gives me the peace afterwards. I know that I'm not being led by hollow, simplistic answers that won't last. I have a God-given conviction that brings continuing joy. Yet I still struggle with how far to go.

"Doing without" has become a part-time hobby for my family. I don't mean to say that we are poor, we're not — we're rich by God's standards. And we don't do without because we somehow get a gruesome kick out of self-denial in and of itself. It is the *giving* that produces the kick, not the denial. When my family can go without a new car knowing that some hungry kids are staying alive instead, that brings joy. And I can forego a new outfit when I know that the proceeds are going to support a missionary to Asia. My family happily eats lots of rice, knowing that it releases more money to give away to others in need. I finally gave my piano away, considering I seldom play it. I don't mean to say that I've conquered materialism. I struggle with these temptations almost every day. I'm still rich. But at least we're headed in the right direction.

Have you been thinking about this subject recently? Has the Lord been dealing with you, too? Is it an issue that keeps popping up here and there? Are you too burdened down by a bunch of stuff which merely makes the journey more laborious? If so, why not start unpacking it and giving it away? Who knows, maybe you'll enjoy the trip much more with a lighter pack!

THE SEDUCTION OF "NICE THINGS"

I like nice things. I know that preaching and writing against materialism is one of my specialties. But, still, I really do like nice things. I like quality, excellent, even luxurious things much more than simply adequate things.

For instance, I like nice cars, especially new ones. I love to ride in one of those high quality automobiles with leather upholstery and deep carpeting. What luxury! And the smell of a new car . . . heavenly! I enjoy feasting my eyes on a brand-new car sitting there with gleaming, still-unmarred paint. Just think how nice it would be to have it. I like nice cars.

I like nice houses too. For years our family rented a tiny 900-square-foot house. Then we settled into a comfortable house quite a bit larger. Best of all, it had a nice two-car garage complete with a large workbench. After years of repairing my car on an open driveway during frigid Indiana winters, having a warm garage was . . . well, "nice." Then we moved again. As we were planning to build our own house, I discovered a basement was "cheap space." I have always wanted a basement where I could play Ping-pong with my sons, maybe even have a workbench where it's warm. So we added a basement in our new house. I like having a basement. It's nice.

I like nice books too. I'm a preacher, so it is part of my job to read and study. When I started out I had three or four shelves of books, mostly my college textbooks and a few used ones I bought from a retiring preacher. Over the years I've accumulated quite a nice collection of religious books, especially on holiness and holy living. I especially like the feel and smell of a brand-new set of commentaries, to say nothing of how impressive they look on my shelf. And, though I know a paperback book is quite as good as the hard-back edition, I much prefer the feel of a nice hardbound book. I love buying books — even more than reading them. Books are nice.

I like nice motels too. In my work I travel a lot. I've stayed in plenty of second-rate motels — the kind where you do your own dusting before you unpack. I've even carried my own can of Lysol a few times. But sometimes I get to stay in a first-class hotel. Oh, I do love it! Everything sparkles so. The towels are so thick and rich, and the beds so firm. There are no leftover hairs on the bathroom floor, and even the tub is fresh and clean. And I love those two little bottles of stuff for your hair. I always keep that cute little sewing kit, and sometimes even the courtesy shoe horn. It's all so . . . well, nice.

Perhaps most of all, I like "toys." I'm a sucker for the things that light up a man's eyes: canoes, chain saws, pick-up trucks, electronic gadgets, and power tools. It's hard to explain to my wife how it feels to go down to my workbench and have exactly the tool I need for the particular job at hand. A few times I have even purchased tools purely on the premise that "someday I'll certainly use that." Men's toys are nice.

What's wrong with liking nice things? Is it wrong to buy a new house, a new car, or some new books? Is it sinful to stay in a nice hotel, or buy a gadget or tool I think I might need?

I wish I had a clear answer to these questions. I struggle with them just about every week. Sometimes I wish there were a list in the Bible of exactly what standard of living was "adequate" and which purchases were luxuries. Sometimes I feel I win over materialism, and at other times I feel I have failed miserably. I wish there were a definite standard of living I could be sure was okay with God. Where's the list when you need it?

There is no list! Not in the Bible or anywhere else! In fact, anyone who makes a list for anybody other than themselves is out of bounds. Jesus gave us *principles* about possessions and left us to apply them ourselves. While these principles do not directly mention things like houses, cars, books, hotels, and gadgets, they were specifically meant to be applied to just such everyday choices.

While I struggle with decisions I make about "nice things," my family has agreed with me on some guidelines concerning these matters. Maybe these will be helpful to you as you hammer out your own family guidelines to resist materialism.

1. Guard against rationalization. It's interesting how my mind works! If I really want something, I can usually figure out a very "spiritual" reason to get it. So, in our family, we bounce purchases off each other to bring us back to reality. If I can get my wife to agree that a new power

tool is really necessary, then I know it really is! The same is true for her when it comes to an electric dishwasher. We keep each other honest in this respect.

2. Watch the trend. Wealth itself is not wrong. It's just dangerous.

Likewise, liking nice things is not sinful, but it can quickly lead to sin. Nice things are seductive. They tend to draw us away from God in tiny "baby steps." It is not wanting *much* that is sin; it is wanting *more*. This is materialism — a constant treadmill of acquisition. We get more only to want *still more*!

The trend of most families today is toward accumulating. In fact, to most the idea of having less at the end of a year than at the beginning seems un-American at best and insane at worst. But it was Jesus who said, "Do not pile up treasures on earth." He didn't say, "Be careful as you pile them up." He simply said, "Do not pile them up."

When the trend in our family drifts toward adding more to what we've got (as it periodically does), then we begin making some decisions about giving away both money and possessions to bring us back into obedience to Christ's command. I don't mean to suggest we are constantly doing this. We seem to gradually pile up stuff for a time, then recognize the trend and unpile a bunch of it, only to eventually gradually pile up some more. The point is, recognize these trends early and do something about them.

3. Watch "big-ticket" purchases. When you are just dying to buy a

big-ticket item, watch out! We have a family rule that all decisions to buy big-ticket items must "marinate" a few weeks. During this time, we try to answer these five questions:

1. Why do we really want it?
2. How will it help us serve Christ better?
3. Could we borrow or rent it?
4. Will it serve *us* or will we serve *it*?
5. What will it cost us to keep it?

It's interesting how some things lose their initial luster under such close examination.

4. When something nice falls into your lap, enjoy it! I am not

calling us all to a life of pain and suffering. Neither am I saying that a life of self-denial will somehow make you godly. Christians are to be joyous

celebrants as well as mourners and sufferers. So if you are generally head-
ing away from a materialistic life, enjoy the trip! If someone gives you
something nice, enjoy it. If you've got a nice house, enjoy it. If God
sends you a power boat, take it, then take a friend water-skiing. When
God serves you the fatted calf, eat what's set before you!

Please don't get the antimaterialism message mixed up with
asceticism.[1] Life is celebration! There are some antimaterialists who
would make you feel guilty for every possession or pleasure you enjoy.
Don't listen to them and ignore their lateral guilt.   They are more like
Judas, who criticized the waste of the perfume for Jesus' feet — "Oh, my,"
they grumble, "that could have been sold for thousands of dollars and
given to the poor." Poor? Sure, poor Judas, that is. So, if you are swimming upstream against a materialistic culture, enjoy the stuff you've still
got left with no guilt. God has not called us to a life of asceticism. If you
are carefully watching the trend of your life, and are constantly increasing
both the amount and the percentage of your giving, then enjoy what
you've kept for yourself without a big burden of guilt. This joy is a special
reward which comes to those who have settled the issue of materialism in
their lives.

5. Remember the purpose. And don't forget the purpose of the sim-
ple life: giving. I have a friend who has a marvelous gift of making
money. Everything he touches seems to turn to gold. He once told me,
"Money is poison; the more I make, the more I'm being poisoned. If I
don't keep sending it out the back door as fast as it comes in the front, it
will kill my spiritual life."

This is the purpose of all this talk about living on less. It is so we can
give more. Give to the needy. Give to those just starting out. Give
anonymously. Give to your neighbor. Give even when you get no tax
credit. Give to your kids. Give to your friends. Give to some college student. Give to your church. Buy a couple of pizzas for the youth group.
Give to your Christian college. Give toward some teen going on a missions trip. Give to help plant a church. Give to keep your camp going
strong. Give to support a missionary. Give a new dress to your pastor's
wife. After all, it's only money.

Do you like nice things? I do. But I can resist the urge to get them
sometimes. Why? So I can give to others. Ironically, there's more joy in
giving than in having.

ENDNOTES:

1. *Asceticism* is a long-standing system of philosophical belief which contends that "practicing strict self-denial is a measure of personal and . . . spiritual discipline." Ascetics, *i.e.*, the practitioners of asceticism, are generally austere in appearance, manner, or attitude, somehow believing that self-denial is both the cause and the evidence of spirituality. The ascetics were and are wrong.

SEX

"The two most common exits from use by God are Money and Sex. If greed doesn't get you, beware of sex."

CHAPTER 5

ANATOMY OF ADULTERY

15 Steps of Unfaithfulness

How does adultery "happen"? People don't just decide one day to hop in bed and be unfaithful to their spouse. Adultery is the culminating act of a dozen or more tiny steps of unfaithfulness. Each step in itself does not seem that serious or much beyond the previous step. Satan draws a person into adultery one tiny step at a time. And he does this over time so that our consciences are gradually seared. This makes it easier to take "just one more step," thinking such a tiny step won't hurt us — "Why, there's no harm in . . . ." Or *is* there? Read on.

The following "15 steps" which analyze how adultery "happens" are based on scores of interviews, counseling sessions, and correspondence with church folk who fell into unfaithfulness. Our question: "How did this happen . . . what were the tiny steps which led to this mess?" While the order varied from case to case, the following is the general progression which surfaced in most cases. This is not some sort of theoretical list. These are the actual steps taken by scores of church people who wound up committing adultery and regretting it later. Some of these people sobbed deeply as they shared, hoping that their own pain and failure might save other marriages. This information comes to you at great expense.

This chapter doesn't have any preaching or analysis . . . that is left to the Holy Spirit and you. Here we offer you cold, word-for-word quotes to think about. You and your Sunday school class can draw out the lessons. How did these lives get ruined? How does it start?

1. Sharing common interests

"We just had so much in common; it was uncanny."

"She and I both enjoyed music, and we were attracted to each other."

"He was so spiritually minded . . . I'd been looking for someone to share my spiritual struggles with."

"We both loved horses and started riding together."

"We both shared a burden for the church and especially children's work."

"She was the first woman I'd ever met who liked the outdoors, even hunting and fishing — I was fascinated!"

2. Mentally comparing with my mate

"My husband wasn't interested much in spiritual things, but this man knew so much about the Bible."

"She was slim, attractive, and dressed sharp — quite a difference from my wife who didn't take care of herself much at that time."

"She was so understanding and would listen to me and my hurts — my wife was always so busy and rushed that we didn't have the time to talk."

"My husband just would never communicate — he'd come home from work and just sit there watching TV. I finally gave up on him. Then this man came along who was worlds apart from my husband — he was gentle, loved to talk, and would just share little things about his life with me."

3. Meeting emotional needs

"He understood how I was feeling and offered me the empathy I was hungering for."

"She was there when I needed her."

"My ego was so starved for affirmation that I would have taken it from anyone — I guess that's what started the whole thing."

"No one had ever really believed in me until he came along. He encouraged me, inspired me, and believed so deeply in what I could become."

"My wife was busy with the kids and not at all involved with my work. This girl admired me and treated me like I was really some-body. It felt so good."

4. Looking forward to being together

"I used to dread going to work, but after we started our friendship, I would wake up thinking of how I would see him later that day . . . it seemed to make getting up easier."

"I would think of being with her the whole time I was driving to work."

"I found myself thinking of him as I got dressed each morning, won-dering how he would like a certain outfit or perfume."

"I looked forward to choir practice every week because I knew he would be there."

"Every time I drove by her house I would think of her and how we'd see each other that Sunday."

5. Tinges of dishonesty with my mate

"When my wife would ask if she was with the group, I'd pretend I couldn't remember . . . right there I started building a wall between us."

"I would act like I was going to practice with our ensemble, but actu-ally I was practicing a duet with him."

"Once my wife asked about her, but I denied everything, after all, we hadn't done anything wrong yet. Now I see that this was one of those exit points where I could have come clean and got off the road I was speeding down."

"Whenever we got together as couples, I would act like I didn't care about him, and afterward I would even criticize him to my husband. I guess I was trying to hide my real feelings from my husband."

6. Flirting and teasing

"I could tell from the way she looked at me. She would gaze directly into my eyes, then furtively glance down my body then back into my eyes again — I knew then that she was interested in more than my friendship. But, I was so flattered by her interest that I couldn't escape."

"Then we started teasing each other, often with double-meaning kind of things. Sometimes we'd tease each other even when we were together as two couples. It seemed innocent enough at first, but more and more we knew it really did mean something to us."

"We would laugh and talk about how it seemed like we were 'made for each other' so much. Then we'd tease each other about what kind of husband or wife the other one would have been if we'd married each other."

"He had those killer eyes. When he'd look at me in that 'special way,' I would just melt. It was hopeless fighting my urges — he had me."

7. Talking about personal matters

"We would talk about things — not big things, just little things which he cared about, or I was worried about."

"We'd meet together for coffee before church and just talk together."

"I was having problems with my son, and she seemed to understand the whole situation so much better than anyone else I talked with. I'd tell her about the most recent blow-up, and she would understand so well. We just became really deep friends — almost soul-mates. That's what's so weird about all this — we never intended for it to go this far."

"I had lost my dad just before we got to know each other and he had lost his mother a few years earlier. He seemed to understand exactly what I was going through and we would talk for hours about how each of us felt."

"I was so lonely since my husband died and hungry for someone to share life with. Then he began to call just because he cared. I loved hearing his caring voice at the other end of the line, even though I knew he was married."

"We spent so much time together at work that I swear she knew more about me than my wife ever did — or even cared to know."

8. Minor yet arousing touch, squeeze, or hug

"He never touched me for months. Then one night after working late, we were walking toward the door when he said, 'You're so special. Thanks for all you do . . .' Then he turned and hugged me tenderly, just for a second. I loved how I felt for that moment so much that I began to replay it over and over again in my mind like a videotape. Now I know that I should have stopped it all right then. I never intended to ruin my family like this."

"She was always hanging around our house and was my wife's best friend. Often she would stay late to watch TV, even after my wife went to bed. She would sit beside me on the couch and I was drawn to her like the song says . . . like a moth to the flame."

"He would often pat me on the shoulder — you know, in appreciation for a good job I'd done. But I knew it meant more than that."

"The first time she touched me was when we were doing registration together. We were sitting beside each other. I'd say something cute or funny, and she would giggle, then under the table she'd squeeze the top of my leg with her hand. That was really exciting to me."

"Every time she shook hands with me at the door she seemed to linger, sort of holding my hand more than shaking it. No one else would notice, but I knew there was more to her touch than appeared to the eyes. She knew too."

9. Special notes or gifts

"He would write these little encouraging notes and leave them in my desk, pocketbook, or taped to my computer. They didn't say anything which could be traced. If anyone found them they wouldn't suspect anything. But we both knew what was going on — we just didn't want to stop yet."

"I would sometimes call him and leave a short message on his answering machine. He would leave little notes in my Bible."

"He would buy me a little gift — not that expensive, but it always showed he had taken extra thought to get exactly what I liked. Of course everyone else thought he was just being a good boss."

"She started leaving unsigned notes to me in my desk sharing her feelings for me. It scared me at first, because I thought someone would find one. But after a while I found myself looking forward to the next one, even though I knew the risk."

10. Inventing excuses to call or meet

"I started figuring out ways I could drop off something at her house when her husband was gone. He and I knew each other and I would always return borrowed tools in the afternoon when I knew she'd be there alone."

"I would wait until the end of the workday; then I'd call him just before closing time about something I'd made up as a 'business question' and we'd talk."

"The more entangled we got, the more I planned times where he and I could practice together. We started meeting more often."

"She started arranging her schedule so that her husband dropped her off at committee meetings. I would hang around and offer to take her home, acting with as much nonchalance as I could muster up."

11. Arranging secret meetings

"By now we both were so far gone that we started meeting secretly at the mall parking lot. I know now how foolish this was, but I was driven by something other than good sense at that time."

"We started arranging to work evenings on the same nights, then we would leave early and meet each other in the dark parking lot."

"I started making sure he knew my travel schedule so we could attend the same conferences. We still weren't involved physically at that time, but there was such excitement and romance to it all . . . even the secrecy seemed to make it more exciting."

"She would sometimes call me just before lunch and we'd sneak through a drive-up together, and then spend the rest of my lunch hour talking quietly to each other."

12. Deceit and cover ups

"Once we were meeting secretly I had to invent all kinds of stories about where I'd been to satisfy my wife. By now I had built a towering wall of dishonesty between us."

"Pretty soon my whole life was full of lies. I'd lie about where I was going, where I'd been, and who I'd been with. The more suspicious my husband got, the better liar I became. But he knew something was going on. It's hard to lie without people suspecting it."

"I joined several groups so that I would have an excuse to be away in the evenings."

"She would ask when I'd gotten off work. I'd simply lie about it, and she never knew what hit her. How can I ever regain her trust now?"

"We agreed that if anyone saw us driving around we would both tell the same story: that my car wouldn't start, he stopped to help, and we were going together to get a new fuse to replace the broken one he'd discovered."

"By now my whole life was a lie, so I began telling them regularly to cover up our little meetings."

13. Kissing and embracing

"The whole thing seemed so exciting by now. I was such a fool. We were meeting secretly and both of us were fearful of being caught. But that only seemed to increase our common ground. When we'd meet, we would embrace as if we'd not been together for years — like in the movies when someone comes home from the war."

"Once we started meeting secretly the end came fast. We kissed and hugged like two teenagers going parking for their first time."

"It just felt so good to be hugged and loved by somebody who really cared about me."

14. Petting and high indiscretion

"At this point my glands took over. I forgot reason altogether and was willing to risk everything for more."

"It was like I was a teenager again — going too far, then repenting and promising to do better; then just as quick I was hungrily seeking more sin."

"When my husband and I were dating we struggled with 'how far to go.' Well, here I was again struggling over the same issue. Friendship with this guy didn't seem so wrong. But now we were going further than I ever intended. But I felt curiously justified going exactly as far as I had with my husband when we had been dating. In a way, I think some of my resentment against my husband's constant pressure on me started coming out. I'm not saying that it wasn't wrong. Just that I kind of felt justified."

"At about this time I began fooling myself into thinking I was heroic for not going 'all the way.' That's what I wanted to do. But by doing 'everything but' I fooled myself into thinking I was successfully resisting temptation. What I didn't realize was that, not only was what I was doing wrong, but that eventually I would also take the next step. It's just not possible to freeze a relationship — you have to go ahead with it, or break it off totally."

15. Sexual intercourse

"Soon I quit resisting and was swept into outright adultery."

"One thing led to another and finally we ended up in bed with each other."

"Though we never intended it to go that far, we eventually went all the way and had sex."

"One night we couldn't seem to stop ourselves (at least we didn't want to) so I completed my journey of unfaithfulness to my husband — I had sex with this man."

If you summarized the advice these people would probably give, what would you say?

CHAPTER 6

How To Protect Yourself From Sexual Sin

*T*he church should be alarmed! I don't mean "disturbed." And I don't mean "concerned." I mean we should be *outright alarmed*! The devil is making gigantic strides into the homes of Christian people. He has doubled his assault on men and women in the area of sexual sin. It is time to talk about it.

I don't like to write about this subject. I like to talk about lofty things like discipleship, holiness, commitment, and leadership. But I am forced to write about sexual sin. How can we have a great revival movement for God when some of our most promising leaders cannot control their own carnal desires? Where is our credibility with the world if the church is caught up in the same sins as they are?

Hardly has a month gone by in the last ten years that I have not bumped into one or more cases of sexual indiscretion among ministers and key laymen of the church. I know what you're thinking. *We have always had this sin among us.* But it seems to me there is a serious outbreak among us recently. Some of these cases are serious indiscretions, some are "minor" indiscretions, but many are acts of outright adultery.

The devil is a liar. No one falls in this area without believing some of the devil's lies. God tells the truth. His Word is light, not darkness. The devil may be multiplying his attack on Christians because he has access to modern "weapons" such as network TV, movies, videos, sexually oriented advertising, cable and satellite TV. He serves these stimulants daily in the living rooms of the average Christian . . . especially those who "watch TV to unwind."

This chapter is written with a heavy heart. I am not that old, but I have seen many dozens of my fellow ministers and key laymen "go down the drain" because of this carnal cancer. Some were the most promising young leaders we had. Others were the steady "salt of the earth" kind of reliable pastors. One recent incident which came to my attention involved a man almost ready to retire who had carried on an affair with a woman for several years before being found out. Just today I read a letter from this broken man. I can't stand quietly by while more fall off the cliffs clinging to this sin and ruin their lives, their marriages, their ministries, and their families!

I recognize that sexual temptation comes to men and women alike. But as a man, I am especially concerned for other men. Some of what I will write here can be equally applied to women. Other thoughts may need adapting for women.[1] If you are a married woman reading this, you probably ought to talk about this matter with your husband sometime. But especially to men, my advice is this:

1. *DON'T START ANYTHING!* I am convinced that adultery usually starts innocently. A man and woman are attracted to each other, maybe even on a "spiritual level" first. Maybe you work together, sing in the choir together, or she is your best friend's wife. You both understand each other so well. You have so much in common and you enjoy quiet conversation with her. She seems more eager to listen than your wife.[2] Soon there are special little words or phrases spoken softly between you. These lead to an "innocent pat," a grateful squeeze of her arm, a meaningful glance, a lingering gaze, a quick hug, a short embrace and . . . eventually you wind up in bed with someone you never intended to defile.

Don't start up this ladder of affection with anyone other than your wife. "Can a man scoop fire into his lap without being burned?" (Proverbs 6:27-29). If you are involved at any stage of affectionate expression, you are playing with fire. Stop, turn around, and turn back.

Please don't misunderstand me. I am not calling for men to be cold, distant, uncaring "icebergs" when it comes to women. You *know* what I am talking about. You don't need anyone to tell you "how far you can go" with anyone else. The Holy Spirit is not on vacation. He will prick your conscience if you are headed the wrong way or if sexual coals are being fanned. *You* will know it. If you are "climbing the ladder" with someone and it is titillating, get off. *Now*! Don't think you can play around with this delectable temptation any longer. The best time to stop disobedience is always today. Tomorrow it will be much harder to do so.

2. *Listen to your wife's advice.* God seems to have given women the special ability to "intuit" and even identify a "strange woman." If you are married, listen to your wife's advice. If she notices or even senses a particular woman "coming on to you," welcome her alerting advice. Don't blow up and call her "paranoid" or "jealous." Listening to her may save your marriage and spiritual life. My wife alerted me several times that she "felt funny" about a particular woman. The first two times I doubted her, but followed her advice to "steer clear." Interestingly, in both of these cases, the woman later got involved in immorality with other married men. How'd Sharon know that? *Wives know!* Maybe God tells them. (Why didn't He tell me?) Anyway, I've learned to listen.

3. *Tell on other women.* If a certain woman begins to quietly come on to you, tell your wife that day. Don't wait until the next morning . . . tell her before you sleep again. She is the most important partner in helping to protect your marriage. Don't start by saying, "I need some accountability with some other guy," when it comes to this matter. You might. But start by telling your wife. You are in this marriage together and both of you must together learn to protect your relationship with each other and with God.

If you are a spiritual leader — especially a minister — you must take special care to follow this advice. Some women may be attracted to your power, prestige, standing in the community and spiritual insights. There may be a woman right now, especially one whose husband is not committed, who is thinking, "If only my husband would be like him." This is wildfire, and it makes you especially vulnerable to temptation. STEER CLEAR! And when you spot someone "melting" toward you, tell your wife. She has as much to lose as you do. The quicker you realize that you are together trying to protect the marriage, the better.

4. *Don't spend time alone with the opposite sex.* Probably enough has been said about this in other places, but let me add, "He who meets another woman alone in private hath no brains." If you are counseling another woman, make sure somebody is in the outer office. If your wife is your partner in ministry, maybe you could counsel another woman as a team. While this is a special warning for ministers, it applies to laymen too. I am surprised at how many marital indiscretions or acts of outright adultery among laymen have sprung up out of a relationship established on the premise of "giving spiritual help" or "sharing our problems together." We tell teenagers to avoid parking alone on lonely country roads. We say that they could put themselves in a place of greater temptation. We should take our own advice.

5. *Drink from your own spring* (Proverbs 5:15). The best defense is a good offense. Though it is not a guarantee, "keeping the fire hot at home" is a good defense against sexual temptation. Paul said as much when he told the Corinthian folk, "But since there is so much immorality, each man should have his own wife, and each woman her own husband. The husband should fulfill his marital duty to his wife, and likewise the wife to her husband...do not deprive each other . . ." (1 Corinthians 7).

Full sexual fulfillment in marriage is God's plan. It is a good defense against outside temptation. You and your wife need to recognize this truth and make sure you are not "defrauding" your partner (1 Corinthians 7:5) by providing a dry or boring "spring" at home. Christian marriages should be the most exciting and interesting sexual partnerships known to mankind. Sometimes the church has railed so much about sexual evils that married couples get the idea that their own sexual relationship is somehow shameful or embarrassing. This is a gross misunderstanding of sexuality, and will be transmitted to your children. The best sex is between a Christian married man and wife. If the truth were really known . . . it would make worldly men jealous!

However, do not allow Satan to suggest to you that any lack of fulfillment in your private family life somehow justifies a little sin to make up for it. It doesn't. Marital fulfillment is *God's* plan. Sometimes one partner is slower to develop his or her God-given sexual gifts to their fullest potential. These things take time. Some of you men are simply too impatient with your wife to allow God's plan to unfold. Be patient. Stick to your own "spring," and in time you will have greater satisfaction at home than you could ever imagine.

6. Be aware of "emotional adultery." This is a greater problem for women than men, so it applies more to your wife than you. However, you too need to beware of getting emotionally attached to any woman other than your wife. Emotional bonding can lead to explosive situations where temptation crashes in on you with greater force than you have ever experienced before. Be careful to guard against gaining significant emotional fulfillment from another woman. Such relationships often develop into much more than emotional attachments and usually result in disaster. And, even if they don't lead to something between you and her, it can hinder your own marriage relationship.

Listen to a letter from one man who lost his wife to another man partly through his own emotional attachment (minor changes to protect the individual):

"Now I see how she was hungry to talk to me when I got home —

and I was so tired that I just picked up the newspaper or mail and read it. I never cheated on her, or even did anything wrong. But I allowed innocent relationships to replace our marriage relationship. Now I realize how I allowed my relationship with one particular person to fulfill my need for conversation, for small talk about the ordinary things of life. Then when I came home, they were already spoken and 'released,' and thus I never shared them with my wife. She got the message I didn't care, or took her for granted. She started looking for someone to share the 'little things of life' with. And she found him . . . . Now I've lost her. My life is ruined. It's a wreck."

Need I say more? Emotional attachments are explosive. They can cause another woman to fall in love with you. An emotional attachment can cause you to lose your head and fall for someone else "who seems to understand me so well," or they can cause such deep emotional bonding that you will seem unable to break away. If you are bonding with another woman emotionally, walk away from it . . . before the entanglement ruins you.

7. Get your thought life under control. Holiness is pervasive. God wants to do more than purify our outward deeds and words. God's power is sufficient even to purify a man's attitudes and thoughts. God offers divine power to take captive every thought, making it obedient to Christ (2 Corinthians 10:5). There are some voices which insist that sexual fantasies are "innocent," "acceptable" . . . even "good for you." This is a *lie*! Lust is the label God's Word uses. Impure thoughts are sin. If you are keeping pure your actions toward other women, and you have not uttered even the slightest words of attachment, yet you are guilty of impure thoughts, you are perching on a precarious precipice which leads nowhere but over the brink into deeper and deeper violations of God's commands.

Who do you think you are? Do you believe that *you* will be the first to escape God's law, "As a man thinks in his heart so is he"? Do you think you can play around with "fantasy fire" without burning your soul? Do you believe you can keep God's anointing on your life as you dwell on thoughts of disobedience? I'm not talking about sexual temptation here — you will likely never escape that. I'm talking about *willfully* dwelling on impure thoughts . . . thinking them *on purpose*. This is a sin!

Consider the incredible power of the human mind: it can multiply and produce much from little! It is like a fertile field. If you plant a few bushels of corn, you get back multiplied more bushels of *what*? Corn! If you plant wheat, what will you reap in return? Much more wheat than you planted! If you plant *negative thoughts* in your mind-field, what will you reap? You will eventually get negative results, and your life will turn sour. If you plant *positive thoughts*, you'll reap positive results and attitudes. This is a universal principle recognized by believers and unbelievers alike. Can you see what this means applied to lustful thoughts? If you plant seeds of lust in your thought life, what do you suppose will sprout — and in incredible abundance? Certainly you will reap a harvest of sexual disobedience . . . sooner or later. This is the law of planting and harvesting. "As a man thinks in his heart, so he is."

Please, let me challenge you to bring *every thought* into captivity, making them totally obedient to Christ — 100 percent. If you have been allowing disobedient thoughts to creep into your mind, confess and repent of this sin. Perhaps worse, you are absolutely saturated with these thoughts — perhaps as a habit since adolescence. Recognize where these seed thoughts will lead. Find out what triggers such temptations and starve their sources — certain people, times, memories, places, TV. Begin memorizing Scripture. Get some accountability. Have faith in deliverance . . . this one doesn't come out easily — but God does deliver in this area.

Thousands upon thousands of men and women can testify that there is no sin beyond Christ's cleansing power. God does "mind-renewals" (Romans 12:2)!

8. *Recognize that you'll get caught.* Are *you* involved in a questionable relationship right now? Perhaps nobody knows about it. It's a secret. You may think you are getting away with it. Satan is telling you, "You'll never get caught." You believe you're the exception — you can get away with it. He says a little bit of sin for a season won't hurt you, and no one will ever find out. Listen carefully. Satan is a liar. You *will* get caught.

Sinners have believed they could get away with sin from the beginning of time. Adam and Eve believed it. They got caught. Cain thought he'd gotten away with murder. Cain got caught. Rebekah and Jacob thought they had deceived everyone. They got caught. Joseph's brothers thought their sales agreement with the Midianites cleared them of ever being found out. They got caught. Moses thought he had buried his sin in the sand. Moses got caught. Achan thought the evidence was well hidden under the floor of his tent. Achan got caught. Saul thought Samuel would never find out about a few animals kept back. Saul got caught. David figured a little sin in the privacy of his bedroom would never come to light. David got caught. Ananias and Sapphira thought they'd devised the perfect plot. They too got caught. The principle is simple: *sinners get caught.*

Do you think you can get away with a little sin? Who do you think you are? You will be like every other sinner down through history. You'll be caught. It is a universal law of life: "Be sure that your sin will find you out" (Numbers 32:23). Do you think you can break God's universal laws of life? Do you think you will be the first who gets away with sin?

How will you get caught? Maybe the woman will tell. She may collapse under her burden of sin and blurt out the whole story in confession at some altar or to a friend or minister. My wife and I know this — we've heard these stories. Or maybe someone else may tell. You think no one suspects, but someone somewhere saw you, and they will tell. When you are sinning, Satan fools you into thinking you are invisible. You're not. Someone will see you sooner or later. Or maybe believers will "just know it." Christians have a special sixth sense about "sin in the camp," and they will sense something is wrong. After it all comes out, many will share that they too suspected something was wrong. Maybe you will tell on yourself. The burden of guilt may eventually be so much for you to handle that you will give up and confess to this sin just to find release and restoration spiritually. You may get away with it for awhile. If you do, you will get more and more bold in your sin, and that in itself will make the sin so obvious that you will eventually cause yourself to get caught.

And if none of these things happen, *God* could tell on you. Even if you don't get found out by any of these means, God himself will bring sin into the light. Do you think you can hide from Him? Don't you think He will continue to do what He has always done — *expose sin?* Do you think you will be the first human in history to get away with sin? God may find a godly, Nathan-like prophet and reveal directly to him what you have done. It may take weeks, months, or even years to surface, but sooner or later your sin *will be found out.* You can't hide sin and get away with it. That is the devil's lie. If you are fooling around with sexual indiscretion, you *will* get caught.

I address this matter last because it is Satan's ultimate lie. Is there not enough evidence about us to illustrate that people do not get away with sin? If you are perched on the edge of sexual indiscretion, turn back now. Flee . . . "leave your coat" behind. Recognize the consequences. Eventually you'll be caught. And you, your family, your church, and all your friends will pay a heavy price. The devil promises you all the kingdoms of this world if you will simply bow down and worship at his altar of impure desires. But you can't have it all. God says your sin will find you out and you'll pay the price. And God is Truth.

Listen to this letter (minor changes to protect the individual):

"It all started innocently . . . or at least it seemed so. My ministry kept throwing a certain girl and me together. She was one of the most active lay persons in the church — and we both carried the identical burden for the church people. It all began in common ministry — that's what's so ironic. We worked together, shared together, prayed together, laughed together . . . not just her and me, but in a group. Yet there was an attraction there . . . a spark between us that lit a fire!

"My wife was busy with the kids and her job. She never suspected anything . . . and I was continually around this lay woman. It happened just like you warn — we started 'climbing the ladder' . . . exchanging little pleasantries, meaningful glances, double-meaning kidding, and finally little touches, pats, a squeeze of the hand, a quick hug, all accompanied by very spiritual overtones. It was exhilarating! I'm not saying I wasn't guilty . . . just that sin had such a powerful attraction to me. I wanted more . . . and I was willing to risk anything — everything to get it.

"Well, to make a long story short — so did she. It seemed like I was helplessly being swept along by a river of desire. It was like I was a teenager again — going too far, then repenting and promising to do better; then just as quick I was hungrily seeking more sin. Soon I quit resisting and was swept into outright adultery. All this time I kept up my 'ministry' — I don't think anyone really knew it — that's scary, isn't it?

"Then, it all came crashing down. 'Be sure your sin will find you out' is true. We got 'found out.' Now my life is a shambles. My dreams have shattered at my feet. I've lost my beautiful wife — I loved her all the time and still do. I've lost my wonderful children — oh, how I ache to be with them again. I've lost my ministry — probably forever — what an ache it is to sit in a service without running it. It's all gone . . . .

"My future, my hopes, my dreams, my family, my reputation, my ministry. The devil doesn't show you where the little temptations lead you. The excitement . . . the delights . . . the powerful seductiveness of sin is fleeting.

"If my story can help others, use it without my name. Tell your young men to 'stay off the ladder' and 'drink from their own spring.' Tell them to clean up their thought life. Tell them sin doesn't pay, and sooner or later it will 'find them out.' Maybe the ashes of my dream can teach others to say NO to the devil.

With little hope anymore,"

This chapter is based on this ruined minister's plea. I don't like to write about this subject. But I have done what the young man asked. Need I say more? If this chapter saves just one of you from going over the brink of destruction, it will have been worth it!

Endnotes:

1. *Other thoughts may need adapting for women.* This chapter is written by a man for other men, though many of the principles apply to men and women alike. Men and women are somewhat different in their sexual temptation. Men are more visual and physical; women tend to be more auditory and relational. For example, Satan often tempts men to imagine an actual sex act with a woman — any woman — visualizing the actual physical process as if it were a play or a video. Satan often tempts women to imagine a cozy relationship full of warmth and tenderness, "wondering what it would be like" to be with a certain man. Thus the triggers of such temptation differ. Men may be triggered by seeing something pornographic, while a woman may be tempted through so-called "woman's pornography"— a soap opera or romance novel. Either way, the temptation is toward unfaithfulness to the one single person I have committed my life to be with.

2. *Good listener.* One Colorado psychologist's summary of more than a decade's work counseling "the other woman" argues that the common trait the "other women" all share is "being a good listener."

Keeping The Fire Hot At Home

omance is like a fire . . . without fuel it eventually flickers and dies. While flickering home fires offer no real excuse for unfaithfulness, "keeping the fire hot at home" is a good defense against outside attacks on our marriage.

The following fire-feeding tips could become a mighty wall of defense around your marriage, defending against the devil's attempt to destroy you.

1. *Celebrate your differences.* Opposites attract. Sharon and I are quite different. She is a detailed planner, sometimes planning every meal a full week ahead of time. I sometimes wander in after work, get a snack out of the refrigerator, only to discover I just ate Thursday's dinner! She likes to go to the beach for vacations. I like the mountains. She likes to watch one TV show straight through. I like to watch several simultaneously. She always wants to stop and ask directions when she thinks we are lost. I like to keep driving because "I know it's somewhere over that way."

When we first started dating, a college professor remarked, "Boy, there goes trouble — two bossy people!" The professor was right. The one thing we have in common is both of us like to be in charge. That hasn't made life easier!

But really we're glad we're different. If two people are exactly alike, one of them is unnecessary. Differences are what make marriage interesting. Differences give us an opportunity to compromise. They provide variety in life. How boring it would be to marry yourself. We all know down deep inside that we want our partner to be different.

Keep the fire hot at home by celebrating your differences. Poke fun at yourself. Admire your partner's attributes, rather than attempting to destroy them and remake them in your own image. Marriage is a celebration of differences, not a process of becoming identical.

2. Say "I love you" often. Steve Orendorff tells how he one day walked up behind his wife of 19 years and whispered into her ear, "I love you." Without saying a word, she went over and marked it on the calendar!

Most husbands think they say "I love you" often. Most wives think they hear it seldom. The point is, verbalizing your love creates an atmosphere of security and commitment. If you've got children at home, it's even more important to frequently verbalize your love for each other. They need to hear this secure commitment out loud. But even without kids, if you love him, say so. If you love her, say so. "I love you" is fuel for the home fires.

3. Verbalize your lifetime commitment. This is even more important than saying, "I love you." Do you plan to stick together for life? No matter what? Even if your husband ends up in an accident and becomes a quadriplegic? How about cancer? What if she gains 50 pounds? What if the "feeling" goes away? What if he changes and becomes "different from the man I married"? Will you stick with this different man? How about if you get rich? What would that do to your marriage? Poor? Sickness? Health? What if things got better? Worse? How long will you stay together? As long as you both shall live?

Are you committed for life? Are you *really* committed, or are you just saying so now. If you really are committed for life, tell each other often. Tell others, too. Never let the word "divorce" be said between you, even in an argument. (Unless you say, "Divorce is not an option, so let's work this out.")

Such a constantly verbalized lifetime commitment will feed your marriage fires and have a soaring impact on your sexual relationship. Many folk have never experienced the heights of sexual expression which result from an atmosphere of absolute security. If you're "in this for better or worse," say so often.

4. Keep dating. Romantic dating fuels the fire. Plan something special. Go out to dinner. Buy her roses. Pick him up at his work and whisk him off to a motel. Get a baby-sitter. Plan a day away. Take a mini-escape weekend. If you just aren't into these serendipitous kinds of things, then simply schedule a date on the calendar. If you are too disorganized, then get your spouse to schedule it.

Sure, all this costs money. But why not? Just think what some people will spend on a cheap hooker on the street. Is it true that some men will spend more for a half-hour hooker than you'll spend to date your full-time lover? Remember those dates you used to take? Some of us husbands were willing to spend more to get our wife than we are to keep her. C'mon. Spend it. She's worth it!

Pick something you both like to do for your date night. Women don't always like the same things we men do. Sharon likes to go out for a nice quiet dinner date. My idea of a good time is to pull on an old pair of bib overalls and attend a noisy farmer's auction. If your wife loves hockey, sure, take her to a game. But if she hates it, try to find something both of you can agree on. Or at least take turns. Who knows, maybe someday she'll say, "You know, I've had a hankering to go to an auction lately . . ." Naaaaaah. Better to find something you *both* like.

5. Do little things for each other. It's the little things which show our love. Twenty-fifth anniversary trips to Hawaii are nice, but if you want to make it to year 25, learn to feed your home fires by doing little loving deeds for each other now. Offer to go get that jug of milk when you run out. Put a note in his briefcase or lunch bag. Bring her a bouquet of flowers. Do something little often to show your love.

My wife and I started exchanging a little card in our early thirties. We can't remember how it got started, but one of us did something extra for the other and left a tiny card reading, "Because I Love You." We passed that card back and forth for years before we lost it and had to make a new one. Our "Because I Love You card" has appeared on a clean pile of dishes, a newly changed bed, a line of freshly shined shoes, a washed car, a totally cleaned off workbench, in a display of roses, and in a dozen other places.

Perhaps this is too "mechanical" for you. But the basic idea is still a good one — doing little loving deeds just "Because I love you." These "little things" are like a pile of fast-burning tinder to the home fires.

6. Take care of yourself. You don't have to be a "hunk" of a man or a beauty queen to maintain the fire at home. But doing nothing may get you just that — nothing. Husbands who slump in their chair each night to watch sports, potbelly hanging out all evening, occasionally burping aloud, can't expect their wives to light up at ten o'clock. And neither can wives expect to attract their husband if they shuffle around with straggling hair, worn off make-up, and that old housecoat with last week's egg stains dripping down the front.

You don't have to be handsome or beautiful, but you should *at least try.*

7. Work on inner qualities. Beauty is only skin-deep. No amount
of outer beauty will make up for inner ugliness. But, inner beauty will
compensate for outer looks. Have you ever noticed a couple somewhere
and said to yourself, "How did she ever get *him*?" Or perhaps it was a
quite average-looking man who was married to a startling beauty. Often
these are cases where a marriage choice was made on inner qualities, not
outer ones. The inner qualities of a person last longest in a marriage.

While it is no excuse for letting yourself go physically, your inner qualities can make your home a warm, inviting place to snuggle. If you are a
grouchy, griping, complaining, nagging, argumentative, selfish individual,
no matter how you take care of your body you will be a "royal pain" to
live with! Rather, developing Christlike qualities can make life with you a
joy. Developing inner traits feeds on itself and produces a lifetime of hot
coals.

8. Take time to "debrief" each day. Most marriages don't die a
sudden death. They suffocate slowly, for lack of communication and
attention. Are your lives so busy that you're like "ships passing in the
night"? Is your communication like shift change in a hospital — limited to
passing on vital information and details to the next shift before you rush
off to your next involvement? If so, you probably need to plan a specific
time for "debriefing."

Debriefing is "sanctified time" just for you and your spouse — to catch
up on each other's lives. No wonder some couples after a divorce say,
"We just grew farther and farther apart" — in other words, they spent precious little time keeping up with each other's lives. Debriefing is time you
set apart *without interruption* to share life. Without it a couple eventually
becomes two separate people who just happen to be roommates. They
are, for all practical purposes, "married singles."

In our family we first did debriefing as soon as we got home from work.
We instructed our preschoolers they could not interrupt "unless there was
blood or fire." Later on we did a debriefing walk after the children went
to bed. Later still we did the walk after supper. Sometimes we miss several days in a row, but generally we've stuck to this time-consuming habit
for almost two decades now. Feeding the marriage fires takes time.

9. Keep your expectations low. That's right . . . *low.* Don't expect
a "perfect" marriage. Have you ever seen one? Would you recognize it if

you ever saw it? Why expect it for yourself? Do you think you will be the first man to find the "absolutely perfect woman" — in every single respect? Why do you think your husband should somehow meet all your needs? We're just broken people, all of us.

Too many marriages wind up in divorce because the couple expected too much from their relationship. One of the great ministries the church should take on today is *lowering* expectations from marriage. How about working toward having a *pretty good marriage*?

I'm a preacher. But am I a perfect one? Nope. But I'm a *pretty good* preacher. I am a writer too. But not a perfect one — my final draft still falls far short of perfection. But I'm a *pretty good* writer. My hobby is rock-climbing. I'm no perfect rock climber — I occasionally fall and even chicken out. But, (considering my age and weight) I'm a *pretty good* rock climber.

Get the point? I'm not a perfect husband, and Sharon and I don't have a perfect marriage. But I'm a *pretty good* husband, and we've got a *pretty good* marriage.

Rather than perfect, how about going for a marriage that is good, long, and strong? How about you? Do you have a pretty good marriage? Is it a fire worth keeping going? Could it be that maybe all you've got to do is keep feeding the fire to keep it hot at home? What one thing from the list above should *you* work on?

ENDNOTES:

1. What excites your wife? For ten years we've been asking Christian wives who attended the *Up With Marriage* retreats to anonymously fill out a sheet titled "What turns me on sexually." Here, in order of frequency, are the responses of the wives:

1. My husband's self-confidence
2. Absolute security
3. Settled arguments — unsettled ones are a turn-off
4. Quiet talking
5. Humor
6. Relaxed environment — privacy, no kids, etc.
7. Emotional tenderness between us
8. Kissing
9. Thoughtful gifts
10. Reading the Bible and praying together
11. Romantic surprises
12. Keeping trim — his belly is a turn off
13. When my husband takes charge spiritually
14. Power — when he's in charge of his life

15. Tender glances long before bedtime
16. An evening date

2. What excites your husband? The same ten years we've been asking Christian husbands attending *Up With Marriage* retreats to fill out a sheet titled "What turns me on sexually." Here, in order of frequency, are the husband's responses: (Sorry, wives, we guys have a shorter list — we're not that complex.)

1. When she sometimes initiates sex
2. Skin!
3. When we try new things
4. When she flirts and teases
5. Touching and cuddling all evening
6. Surprising me
7. When she enjoys sex and says so
8. Affirming me — criticizing me is a turn-off
9. Taking care of herself — looking good

CHAPTER 8

CAN A HOMOSEXUAL BE "CURED"?

A guide to thinking through the issue

C hristians cannot ignore the rising number of gay men and lesbian women who insist "we were born this way" and thus God never intended for them to be any other way. They argue, "God made us the way we are." So, for the church to insist they get "cured" is inappropriate, they say.

What do *you* think? Have you thought through the homosexual issue from a biblical and theological perspective? If you've already made up your mind, this chapter won't help much — it will merely reinforce what you already believe or do not believe. However, if you've never thought through the issue theologically for yourself, the following guide may help:

1. Why try to "cure" homosexual behavior?

The first question is whether or not homosexual actions even need curing. If you believe homosexual actions are "normal," or at least "acceptable," then there is no need for you to think much further. If they are normal or acceptable sexual expressions, then they do not need to be changed or abandoned. Do you think this behavior is normal?

If you do, then you've got some fancy footwork to do with the Bible. The teachings of the Bible take a definite stand on homosexual practices. If you are going to be honest in your stand, you will need to develop an adequate explanation for numerous Bible passages which are hard to explain away.[1]

It is difficult for an honest Christian to study the Scriptures and accept homosexual behavior as normal or ordinary. The Old Testament penalties are severe, and the New Testament scriptures consider the practice perversion — even keeping the practitioners from entering God's Kingdom. If you intend to accept homosexual behavior as anything other than sin, you will have to turn somewhere else besides the Bible to prove it. And when you have done that, you have made the Bible a secondary source on the definition of sin, and you have departed from answering the question from a Christian perspective.

Sure, a nice agnostic-humanist might be able to accept homosexual behavior. If you get standards of right and wrong from your own "gut feelings" or from a poll on what the "average person" thinks, then you might accept this behavior as normal and natural. But if you believe the Bible is the source for our definition of sin, you will have a difficult task accepting homosexual behavior. If you stick with the Bible, you'll probably have to call homosexual behavior sin.

2. Do homosexuals have to act on their urges?

Since the Bible condemns homosexual behavior as sin, it is difficult for a Christian to dismiss it. But if you are wishing to accept homosexual behavior among Christians, you may have another option if you are looking for a loophole.

You could adopt a *"forgiven-sin theology" as some homosexuals have done.* They say:

> "We are all sinners... every day, in word, thought, and deed; the only difference between an unsaved sinner and a saved sinner is that the saved sinner has already had all his sins forgiven — past, present and future. I'm only human, and when I fall into homosexual sin, it is a joy to know that God can't see that sin— for all my sins were forgiven past, present, and future — when I became a Christian."

This theology is accepted in some Christian circles, though it is more often applied to more "acceptable" sins than to homosexual actions. If this approach is applied to homosexuality, it allows for homosexuals to become Christians, stay Christians, and practice homosexual behaviors occasionally, but since they are a saved homosexual, the sin was forgiven in advance by God. This doctrine says the Christian homosexual can rejoice that "there is therefore now no condemnation," for their homosexual sin — past, present, and future — was forgiven when they became a Christian.

If you choose this forgiven-sin approach, you need to honestly examine what it does to the rest of your theology. Will you accept *any* sin in the life of a Christian? How about a life *full* of sin? How about a person who regularly practices sin — can he or she still be a Christian? Is sin that inconsequential? Are you willing to say there can be minimal or no difference between a believer's and an unbeliever's life — only a change of *status* before God?

If you honestly choose this forgiven-sin option, your theology might permit homosexual behavior among believers — but can you do it? Can you honestly accept this theory, given the Bible's frequent calls to abandon sin and live a holy life? Can you honestly allow for a Christian to sin purposefully and regularly — even every day?[2] Most sensible Christians believe that Christians can't take that light a view of sin and sinning.

Where does this leave you? If you are (1) not able to dismiss homosexual behavior as normal, since the Bible calls it sin, and (2) you are not able to accept homosexual sin as something God overlooks along with all the other sins we do every day as the "normal" part of the Christian life, what are you left with?

You are probably left with a *theology of victory.* Many sensible Christians are not comfortable with either excusing or overlooking sin. Most assume there is victory available for any Christian struggling with *any* kind of temptation. For the homosexual, it means "You don't have to do it." A victory theology says, "You may have homosexual urges, but you don't have to act on them." In other words, through God's transforming power, a Christian with homosexual urges can live victoriously — he or she can be a "nonpracticing homosexual."

This seems to be such a sensible approach because it is consistent with our treatment of all other sins. Many Christian men are plagued with impure thoughts — they have a strong sexual drive toward other women. But we teach "you don't have to do it." We teach these heterosexual men that even though they were "born with these strong urges," they don't have to act on them — by God's grace they can be faithful all of their lives. To have an urge does not mean you are destined to act on it.

A sensible "victory theology" treats homosexuality the same way. Sure, the homosexual may be born or raised in such a way so that they possess powerful urges for same-sex relationships. But with God's grace, they do not have to act on the urge just because they have it. God's grace is greater than that. The simple quote representing this victory theology is: "If the Bible calls it sin, you don't have to do it." If you end up following this track of thinking, you will expect any Christian who has homosexual urges (or any other sinful urges) to keep from acting on them — to be non-practicing.

But there's a third question you might think about as well.

3. Can a homosexual be "cured" of his or her urge?

This is a deeper and more perplexing question. Can a Christian with homosexual desires be delivered from *wanting* to commit homosexual sin? Is a homosexual Christian stuck with these sinful urges as long as he or she lives on this earth? Is it possible for a homosexual to be "delivered" — not just from the behavior — but from the *inclination* toward homosexual sin?

Some answer with a loud "no." They argue that the inclination toward homosexuality is deeply rooted in the psyche of a person by birth and/or environment. They argue that it is so much a part of the person that they can no more be delivered from homosexual desires than someone can be delivered from left-handedness. These people argue, "I have never heard of a single homosexual cured of the basic drive toward homosexuality, and those who claim to be are lying." These Christians stay with the victory option outlined above, and nothing more. To the homosexual they say, "You can't be blamed for what you are — these desires are a part of who you are — but you don't have to act on them . . . through God's power you can be a Christian nonpracticing homosexual. You might *want* to act on these urges, but you don't have to."

But there is a group of Christians who go one step further. They ask, "Is there more than victory over *wanting* to sin?" They wonder, "Is a Christian with homosexual urges destined to *want* to commit homosexual acts all his or her life?" Could God go a step further? Why couldn't God provide a correction for the bent in a person's nature toward a specific sin? Is it possible that a homosexual could quit *wanting* to commit homosexual sin? Could a homosexual be cured of his homosexual inclination?[3]

Some Christians take this bold "second step" in their theology of victory. They believe that a Christian can become more than a nonpracticing homosexual. They think God can actually deliver or cure the person from homosexual sinful urges. They claim that a homosexual can receive a work from God which changes the homosexual's *nature*, delivering him from all sinful homosexual drives.

Basing their belief on their interpretation of Scripture and sanctified logic, these Christians proclaim that God is at work in every believer not only to act according to His purposes, but also to *will* — to purify a man, or woman's desires. This group claims, "You don't have to sin; and you don't have to want to either."

Using logical thinking along with the Scriptures, they argue that homosexual sin is not so radically different from other sins. They believe each of us is born or raised in such a way as to result in a personal "propensity" for selected sins. Some are more inclined to anger and rage, others to drunkenness, others to resentment, bitterness, or an unforgiving spirit, while still others to heterosexual lust and the urge to be unfaithful to their spouses. They lump homosexual sin right in with these kinds of biological or environmental "besetting sins."

These "second step" folk believe that God can do more than help us gain victory over a sin — He can even deliver us from our inclination to commit that sin.

Take a person who has a powerful sinful heterosexual urge — someone who is constantly plagued with lustful thoughts and fantasies about cheating on his wife. These people say that not only can that man keep from cheating on his wife — i.e. "live victoriously" — but there is also a "second step" available from God which can correct his abnormally strong *desire* to have sex outside marriage. In other words, a man is not stuck with wanting to cheat on his wife as long as he lives. God can perform both a gradual and a complete work in his heart so that he no longer *wants* to cheat on her.

These people are not shocked by a person's confession to homosexual urges. They happily point out that he or she cannot only have victory over the practice of this sin, but can also be delivered from the urge to commit this sin, or any other sin.

Such seekers should be cautioned against any sort of "slot machine cure" where they expect a fast and easy instantaneous deliverance. This kind of cleansing often takes time. It may come only after many months or even years of seeking. But these people argue it *can* come. God's grace can do more than make us "nonpracticing sinners" — people who don't actually do it, but really want to. He can go a step further — actually correcting our unhealthy desire to sin, enabling us to obey Him because we want to.

This "second step" approach to homosexuality is worth examining. Has the modern evangelical church sold itself short on God's transforming power? Can God give total victory over the practice of a sin? And can God give a second touch to a believer which can make him not even *want* to commit a sin? Is there a "double cure" for sin? These second step Christians believe there is. I'm one of them — I believe God can do this. What do you think?

• •

ENDNOTES:

1. For a start see: Genesis 19:5; Leviticus 18:22; Leviticus 20:18; Deuteronomy 23:18; Judges 19:22; and in the New Testament, Romans 1:26-27; 1 Corinthians 6:9.

2. The Bible's treatment of purposeful sin in a believer's life is too extensive to list here, but consider one small book's treatment: 1 John 2:1; 2:5-6; 3:6-9; 3:24; 5:18. Few Christians can read these passages without concluding that those who are habitually practicing purposeful sin with no intention of stopping aren't really Christians at all, and if they claim to be, they are lying.

3. I am not talking here of the *capacity* for homosexual behavior, but the *inclination*. Every human being has the capacity for every sin ever imagined, including homosexuality. If we had no capacity, we could never even be tempted. A capacity to sin is a neutral potential for sin; the *inclination* to sin is an inside "driven-ness" or urge to sin which becomes an inner ally to the Tempter. We can never escape the capacity or potential to commit sin. But certain Christians believe it is possible to escape the inclination or "driven-ness" to commit any sin, including this sin, homosexuality.

CHAPTER 9

MALE SPIRITUALITY

Men are different from women when it comes to spiritual things. Their basic religious nature differs, the way they express spirituality differs, and the process of spiritual life change is different. Yet, we know so little about male spirituality. The truth is, most Christians know more about the difference between male and female sexuality than about their differences in spirituality.

Most churches cheat men spiritually. Modern evangelical religion has been pretty well feminized for more than a hundred years, at least since the American revival awakening period. Evangelical religion is nice and tender, lifting up a kinder, gentler sort of a Christian image for men.

Men are supposed to accept this feminized brand of religion as "new and improved" religious expression. The trouble is, feminized religious experience won't fully meet the needs of men. A steady diet leaves a hole in a man's religious psyche. Demons fill that hole. The man senses something is missing, but he can't quite put his finger on it. Feminized religion won't meet all his needs — especially his deepest spiritual needs.

I can hear it already. Most of my readers are already going up in smoke. I know. The majority of readers of this book are women. The majority of the *church* is women. Plus, women are more inclined to read books than men. (If you are a married woman, and are studying this book for Sunday school class, I suspect you are reading this first and your husband expects you to brief him on the way to Sunday school!) If you are angry with my approach in this chapter, let me explain where I stand.

I'm against feminization of religion. I'd like to see a more balanced view of spirituality pervade the church, or at least we should do something extra to meet the differing spiritual needs of men and women. However, while I'm against the feminization of religion, I'm not against the women's equality movement in the church. I believe women and men should be fully equal in the church . . . women ought to be called into the ministry, ordained to preach, paid equally, and hold about half of the board and administrative positions in the church. I personally have an equality marriage with my wife, and in many ways I am more "feminist" than most women in the church. This chapter is not against the tiny progress women have made in gaining equality in the church. That is not the issue here.

This chapter is about *male spirituality*. It is about the different needs of men when it comes to spirituality. It is about thinking . . . thinking about these differences, and finding ways the church can spiritually lead the 30-35 percent minority of its adults who happen to be men. And it is about reaching out to the vast number of men outside the church.

The feminization of religion probably started in Sunday school for most of us. When you and I were children, most men at the church refused to work with children (many still do). They figured children's work was "woman's work," so a host of dedicated women gave us our earliest and deepest impressions of Bible stories. Men were largely absent or distant.

Without ever intending to do it, these women naturally taught the Bible with a feminine bias. They couldn't help it . . . no more than a man can help teaching with a male bias.

I'm not angry with these dedicated women who feminized our view of religion. Bless them! God will reward their dedicated labor. I'm angry with the men who refused to get in there and teach children's classes, providing a balanced view of Jesus. These men preferred serving on a board so they could decide on the "weightier matters" of theology . . . like how to pave the parking lot. They passed up the work of becoming a spiritual "male mother" to us Junior boys. Most of us got women teachers, and a feminized view of religion came along with them.

Face it, we were raised on the "Sunday school Jesus," a softer nicer version of the real Son of God. We met a Jesus who was a nice boy . . . sweet, soft, mild, quiet, "vanilla." He was polite, always closed the doors after himself, obeyed His mom, always took a bath. He smiled sweetly, shared His crayons, talked softly, but never carried a big stick. This cozy Jesus never caught a butterfly — He just watched them, according to the pictures we were shown. He helped His mother, cleaned up His room, never wiggled in church, said nice things to people, and evil *men* in a mob said "Crucify Him!" (Go ahead, check the scenes on most pictures — *men* did it!)

It was not just the teachers, but the writers and editors too. I suppose it is no secret that 90 percent of all children's curriculum editors are women (in many denominational offices it is 100 percent). That is why almost all — perhaps all — Sunday school curriculum for children has been feminized. Can you blame these women for having a feminized view of Jesus?

No. But because of the inequality of our culture, any man who becomes a children's editor will almost automatically "move up" into administration within a year or two and thus will no longer directly affect the week-by-week work on curriculum. That leaves women editing the children's curriculum as well as teaching it.

I know. I've sat on these committees off and on since 1978. I remember one committee where one lonely man argued vehemently to include in the Junior curriculum "the whole story" of David and Goliath — right down to cutting off Goliath's head. He lost, of course. These editors liked the harp-player better than the warrior. The final compromise: the story would end with the stone hurtling toward Goliath, since a third of the women even wanted to omit the actual stones hitting Goliath. This is just one of hundreds of illustrations of how the Bible has been "cleaned up" by editors to support a "nice Bible" which produces "nice kids." Most of us were imprinted early with this "cleaned-up Bible" based on a feminized curriculum.

What we got of the New Testament was just as biased. These editors and teachers confused the nature of God — which is neither male nor female (or, perhaps *both* male and female) — with the nature of Jesus, who was, in fact, a man. For most of us, the Jesus we got was androgynous — both feminine and masculine. This feminized Jesus is the dominant imprint many Christian men still have. Almost all worldly men have it too. In short, Jesus was the sort of boy every mom could hope her son would turn out to be . . . but the dad might be disappointed. Most of us still think of Jesus in this way.

Is this why most men feel so unspiritual? It's true! Most men live with terribly low spiritual self-esteem. Ask a group to bow their heads and raise their hands if "my wife is more spiritual than I am." Every time you'll get 70 to 80 percent raising their hands (unless, perhaps, they've read this chapter). I've done it over and over with the same results. Is it true? Are women really more spiritual than men? Did God *make* men more evil? Or, could men just *think* they are less spiritual? Could they be comparing themselves with a feminized picture of Jesus and losing out? Are they saying, "Nope, I'm not much like Jesus . . . my wife's more like Him." Are they measuring themselves against a biased view of Jesus? Have they been permanently imprinted by the "Sugar-Jesus" of Sunday school? Do the "snakes, and snails, and puppy dog tails" in their own life constantly remind them that they aren't "Christlike" like their wife or girlfriend? Most men have such a feminized view of Jesus that they believe most unsaved women are more Christlike than many saved men.

What is a "Christlike man" anyway? For many men he is merely the grown-up version of the Sunday school "nice boy." He is sweet, soft, cozy, likes quiet talking, and doesn't walk on the grass. The good Christian man dresses nicely, attends Sunday school, sings in the choir, drives slow, wears a tie, shows up, picks up after himself, and is trained so well that he always puts the seat down.

Face it, even our view of sin is warped. Ask 100 Christians to list "Ten serious sins." Then ask a totally different group to make two lists: "Ten temptations of men" and "Ten temptations of women." Every time you'll discover the same thing. There will be amazing overlap between the "Ten serious sins" and the "Men's temptations." Christians generally consider men's sin more "serious" than women's sin.

Is it true? Are men *made* by God to want to do the "bad" sins, and women are more inclined to commit the "better" sins?

Or, is our *view* of sin warped? Has the church harped primarily on the sins of men and downplayed the "lesser" sins toward which women are inclined? Is this why men harbor such deep feelings of shame?

Take ministers, for instance. Has the church adopted the media's own feminized view of ministers? Ministers should always be soft, and sweet, and nice. The media stereotype of a minister is a religious gelding . . . a nicely dressed, sissified fat man who likes to drink tea with old ladies. When was the last time you saw a minister on TV hunting, or playing football? Ministers are the "eunuchs" of today's society. In fact, many ministers seem to leave their masculinity behind when they enter the pulpit. This is how feminized the church, and clergy, have become. But these men know they are missing something, but they can't put their finger on it. It is their manhood.

Enough about feminized religion and its effect on males. The effect is so deep and so early that most men do not even recognize it, and will heartily deny it. In fact, many feminized men cannot accept the ideas in this chapter. Their concept of Jesus and Christlikeness is so permanently feminized, and their manhood is so suppressed, that their mind automatically filters out any idea that Jesus was anything different from "sugar and spice and everything nice."

Many Christian men feel inadequate, and sense that they lost something somewhere along the way, but they just don't know what it is. They lost their own manhood. In becoming "Christianized" they thought they had to give up being a man and become more like their mothers and their wives. So these men lose touch with a primary avenue of spiritual progress — their own manhood.

. . . .

Male Spirituality

What is male spirituality anyway? Does male spirituality differ from feminine spirituality? I don't know for sure. These thoughts are preliminary, but based on interviews and discussions with several hundred men. How might male spirituality differ? It seems some of these characteristics are different:

Male spirituality is more aggressive. It is not passive and quiet. The deepest spiritual expressions of a male are hard, heavy, even violent. This fearsome spirituality, when unleashed, is scary and makes most men shut off their feelings —spiritual feelings — and appear cool and aloof when it comes to spiritual matters.

Male spirituality is "visual-spatial." Words are less important to men than seeing. Even in their sexuality men prefer seeing. That is why "skin magazines" make it with men, but not as much with women. Some argue this visual-spatial edge is why males consistently score higher in the math section of aptitude tests.[1] For whatever reason, men are more "visual." They love stories.

In their natural state, men trade hunting stories, jokes, and swap yarns — visual pictures. Male spirituality is more driven by stories and parables than by lists and details. A story or drama communicates better with men than a ten-point "How to" message. This was how Jesus communicated.[2]

Men are less relational and more physical-mechanical. They would rather *do* something than have a cozy chat. What does this say about 90 percent of the church schedule? Most churches are primarily designed for listening and sharing. We schedule lessons to talk about witnessing, but we don't actually go out and do it during Sunday school. Men stutter more frequently, and talk 40 percent less than women on any given day. They'd rather *do* than talk. In fact, doing something is their dominant form of spiritual expression, not religious talking and listening. This is why men's lives change more on a five-day missions work team than sitting quietly through a hundred Sunday services.

Men are often more informal, especially in their dress. While corporate America has pretty well trained men to "get up, dress up, and show up," even many of these corporate guys can't wait to get home and get out of their "monkey suits." Many men don't like to dress up. Go ahead and find 100 men in their natural nonbusiness settings — how do they dress? Compare that with how we expect people to dress at church, especially ministers. I know, "God deserves our best" and all that, but go door-to-door inviting men to church and you'll hear how often many of them

• •

resist the idea of getting up next Sunday to put on their "funeral suit." And I know, the church is always saying, "You can come any way you'd like here." But how the leaders dress on the platform is what we *really expect.* Face it, we've designed the church for men and women who like to dress up.

Men are warriors. They possess a tremendous amount of pent up warrior energy.   When released properly it can result in aggressive decisive action.   When this energy goes awry the results are devastating.   The proper release of "warrior energy" in a man's spiritual expression is an opportunity most Christian men never get.   However, most modern men relate better to King Saul than to the warrior David.   The warrior is committed to a cause above himself — an idea, a concept, a principle.   And he is willing to die for it.   In fact, the imminence of his death makes the warrior-man willing to risk all for something greater than himself.   We church leaders more often recruit men to enlist as religious bureaucrats then Christian soldiers.   But male spirituality yearns for a call to arms, hungers for a Christian General Patton to inspire him to aggressive life-risking action in behalf of a cause bigger than himself.

Men carry deep grief. Grief is not exactly the right word for it, but it's the closest word to explain the concept. Sure, women grieve too, but men carry a great burden of *unexpressed* grief. Anyone who has retreated with an all-men's group knows it. Grief comes pouring out like blood from a wounded side. Could it be from the inherited memory we have of generations of killing?   Do we somehow carry thousands of years of collective memory of death within us? Wars. Hunts. Who knows? But it is there. Men sometimes are somber, pensive, noncommunicative, and sad down deep inside.

Yet today's religion is mostly a cheery "feel-good" experience. We figure that's how we're supposed to run the church: "Aren't you glad to be here on this beautiful day? Turn and shake someone's hand and tell them that you love them," says the Reverend Mr. Cheerleader. We men dutifully turn, shake, and smile. But we sometimes feel like hypocrites. Some days we aren't cheerful. We're not glad about anything. We grieve. This is not just one personality type — it is the common experience of *all* males. The answer to our spiritual quest is to go downward into the grief, and not upward into celebration. There's not much room in today's religion for someone to go down. All routes lead "up."

If a man admits his grief, the church will pray for him so he can "get over it." Down is "bad," up is "good." Feeling good is what most churches are all about. But men know you can never "get over it" — not the essential grief which is so much a part of men's psyche. Grief is part of

• •

our nature — our *spiritual* nature — and we need to express it, not recover from it. But how should we express it?

Because of their acquaintance with grief, men intuitively understand the cross. In fact they are fascinated by it. Men also relate to the "unchristian" parts of the Old Testament, even to what seems to be the "unchristian side of God" in the Old Testament. Most men carry a grief which has no vehicle for expression in the cheery "sunny" evangelical religion of today. So they leave their grief buried deep within and act happy. But it's still there, and somehow it's related to their spirituality and needs to find expression.

Men are earthy. (Women say we are "gross.") Who knows why? Maybe it's our "raw material" — we were made from the earth itself. It seems as if men yearn for the dirt they were made from. Why aren't women earthy? Who knows? But they usually aren't. They started with something alive — a rib — and the rest must come from high up somewhere else — maybe from heaven itself. Or, perhaps it has nothing to do with our creation. Perhaps it is due to how we raise our kids. For whatever reason, boys and men tend to be earthy. Anyone who has spent more than a day with an all-men's group will testify to this earthiness of men!

Is there any place in the church for the "earthy side" of men? Is there an earthy side to the Bible? Who will tell teenage boys this side of the Bible? Who will help them understand how to channel this part of their natural being into Christian expression? Or, will they learn that to become a good Christian a man has to deny his earthy side, and become more like a woman?

Men are reckless risk-takers. Ask the insurance companies. Men take chances. They are rash and competitive, especially so when they are young. Men even risk their lives more often than their female counterparts. Men do stupid things — or at least what civilized folk think is stupid.

How does this risk-taking inclination affect a man's spirituality? How would your church react to a man who quit his well-paying job this week, uprooted his wife and two kids, gave away his house, and took his family off to Alaska to "witness to the Eskimos"? Most of us would believe he'd gone off his rocker. But wasn't this kind of risk-taking just about what Jesus called the rich young ruler to do? Or what about Abraham? The rich ruler couldn't take the risk. He was a half-man. Abraham was different. So was Peter. A real man sometimes walks away from his nets. Real men take "foolish risks" sometimes. Does the church fan the flames of this side of men's spirituality? Or, do we train them to be good little men and behave themselves in the cozy little routines of home and church?

Men are wild. In fact, this may be their dominant trait. Even the corporate man has a wild streak deep inside. The corporation has contained it, but he sometimes lets it out after work. This wild streak makes men unpredictable, untamed, maybe even dangerous at times. Every man has a wild man inside him. For many, it is deep below the surface, and chained up by years of training. But even the most domesticated Christian man knows he's got a wild man deep within. When the wild man is released, it results in action, sometimes life-risking action, and often an almost superhuman fury and energy.

Most of us men have been taught that the wild man is evil . . . that it is really our carnal nature, dressed up like a wild man. But this is false. The real wild man is Jesus! It is the real Jesus. Not the Jesus we've been taught about as a child. It is the Jesus who refused to let people put Him in a box. It is the untamed Jesus. The unpredictable Jesus. This Jesus caused trouble everywhere He went. He broke the Pharisee's Sabbath rules. He treated women like equals in a society which treated them as possessions. He told the status seekers they would be last in the Kingdom. He railed against the crooked religious bureaucracy. He told people their preoccupation with detailed rules was silly, and He replaced the rules with broad-stroked principles.

This wild man Jesus fought with the devil, declared war on organized religion, and left home and wandered around a couple of years with a group of other guys. This is the wild man Jesus they never told us about. This is the Jesus who knew what it meant to say, "Happy are those who mourn." This is the Jesus who seldom said what people expected. This is the Jesus who withered a fig tree with His anger. This is the Jesus who turned over tables in the Temple as He angrily whipped a herd of animals ahead of Him. This wild man Jesus got himself killed. For you.

Are you a Christian man? If so, this wild man Jesus lives inside you. Perhaps you have repressed His wild side. Of course, you have. You've been taught to do it. But He is there nonetheless. Every man, sooner or later, has got to release the wild side of Christ. Not unleash evil, mind you. Christ never does that. But to release a spiritual fury you know lurks beneath the surface in your inner man. This wild man Jesus can lead you into a new liberated level of masculine spirituality. Release Him and let Him go!

A final thought:

This chapter is, of course, controversial. It is not a completed work . . . it's preliminary. You may disagree with all or most of it. You may say,

"Women are like that too in one or another of the characteristics." Or you might say, "I don't think men and women are any different spiritually." Of course you think this way. *Everyone* thinks that way now. But is it true? The real issue is not whether men are different in the specific ways I mentioned above. Some of these observations may be accurate, and others faulty. The real issue, the essential question, is: *Are there any differences in male and female spirituality?*

If you think there may indeed be some differences, for whatever reasons, then the next obvious question is: "How should we consider these differences in our church's ministry to men?"

My hunch is that there are differences, and we are largely ignorant of (and maybe terrified by) male spirituality. It's worth thinking about . . . and talking about. Someone ought to write a book on this subject.

ENDNOTES:

1. This chapter does not deal with whether the differences between male and female are a result of nature or nurture. Perhaps some differences are birth differences, others are developed in the environment, and some result from a combination of both. Discussing *why* men and women may be different is not the issue; the real issue is *Are* they different? If they are indeed different, then the church must consider these differences, at times providing specialized, intense ministry to singles, the aged, women, couples, *and men too.* Lumping everyone together is fine most of the time — but specialized needs cannot always be met in the "lump." And even in the lump, some consideration must be given to male spirituality so there is a more balanced view of Christlikeness.

2. Jesus' communication style was almost completely masculine, but His culture and His audience were almost totally dominated by men. We need both styles today.

3. I am not suggesting that men exclusively possess the warrior trait, just that for thousands of years this has been a particular characteristic of men. And I do not suggest that women like Mary Slessor, Dorothea Dix, and others are not great warriors — in fact, there is an increasing number of female warriors today . . . just as men are passing them the other way as they become more feminine.

PART THREE

SPIRITUAL POWER

"The source of spiritual power is in an obedient walk of intimacy with Christ — you can't get that at a seminar."

CHAPTER 10

NINE THOUGHTS ABOUT TEMPTATION

When will temptation stop? Is there ever a point in your spiritual life when you will get beyond temptation? Will you ever be delivered from Satan's persistent attacks? Can you hope for rest sometime in the future from ensnaring temptations?

No. It is no use misleading you. You will be continually tempted to sin throughout all your life. So, if you're stuck with temptation, you might as well learn how to beat it. There are some basic truths about temptation which, if you know and apply them, will help you defeat the devil:

1. GREAT TEMPTATION OFTEN FOLLOWS "SPIRITUAL HIGHS"

The devil is sly. He knows we are especially vulnerable to his attack after we have "come down" from a great "spiritual high." Take Jesus, for example. He came to be baptized by the most famous evangelist of the day, John the Baptist. John recognized Him as the Messiah. As He was being baptized, Jesus actually heard God's voice from heaven, and the Spirit descended on Him. Quite a spiritual high!

What happened next? He went directly into the wilderness and was tempted for 40 days by the devil (Matthew 3,4). The devil does not tempt at random. He tempts as part of a comprehensive strategy. He knows our emotions are especially vulnerable following a spiritual high time.[1] Perhaps we have let down our guard.

What to do? Watch for these attacks after retreats, camps, conventions, revival meetings, or special services. Immediately following the times when things are going great, the devil drags out his biggest cannons of temptation. For me temptation is often absent or suppressed while I'm having a great meeting or revival. But I've learned to get ready for an attack the moment I get into the car or plane and head home. I may have made a fabulous crossing of the Jordan River — but just inside I come face-to-face with the towering walls of Jericho. Watch out for a big temptation right after a spiritual high.

2. GOD SOMETIMES LEADS US INTO TEMPTATION

Although God never tempts us (James 1:13), He does *lead* us into places where the devil can tempt us. Even Jesus was led "by the Spirit" into the wilderness to be tempted (Matthew 4:1).

Why does God do this? It almost seems like God and the devil are somehow cooperating in a diabolical plot. Why? Because God sees temptation as a "test." Luther was once asked what he thought was the best preparation for the ministry. His one-word answer: "Temptation." God knows that the greatest training for overcoming temptation is . . . overcoming temptation. The more often we refuse to give in to the devil, the stronger we will be in the future.[2] So, God sometimes leads us into a place where the devil will tempt us so that we can resist and become stronger.

Now, don't get me wrong here. A lot of temptations we face, God had nothing to do with. Sometimes, we lead ourselves into temptation! But, still God sometimes leads us to a place where our resistance can be trained and strengthened. We fear this fact about God — so much so that we pray, "Lead us not into temptation." But knowing that God does indeed lead us into temptation at times, we follow that quickly with "But, deliver us from evil." God knows that repeated experiences in resisting temptation will strengthen our will and make us stronger than ever.

But there is another truth which encourages us: He will never let us be tempted in a way which we will be unable to resist (1 Corinthians 10:13). There are some temptations which, if we faced them now, we would certainly "cave in" to and sin. We are not yet strong enough to resist them. But God will not allow these temptations to come our way. In fact, if we are being tempted, we know for sure that God has already approved that temptation to come our way. He has already decided that we are strong enough to resist it.

So the next time you're tempted, keep in mind that God has not lost control of the game and somehow the devil has "blindsided" Him. Rather this temptation has been "approved" by God to be sent my way — for God knows that I'm strong enough to beat it, with His help. To God, it's a test or training for me. And when I do overcome, I'll be stronger for it!

3. THE DEVIL TEMPTS US AT OUR WEAK POINTS

Satan isn't stupid. He does know all things, but tempting is his game, and is one of his names. He and his invisible demons recognize our strong and weak points. It would be foolish for him to continually attack you at an area where you are strong! He doesn't need to read this chapter to know that the more you resist temptation, the stronger you'll get. If he continually attacked you at your strong points, you would merely resist repeatedly. This repeated victory would produce great spiritual power for you!

So, Satan attacks at your weak points — the points where you are most likely to give in. This way he has the best chance of beating you. He finds a weak link in your chain, a soft spot.[3] He often tempts through your natural, God-given desires by suggesting that you pervert them for wrong purposes. For instance, sex is a good, God-given drive, but God wants unmarried people to wait until marriage, and married individuals to focus all their sexual energy on their spouse.

The way to discover your own weak point or "besetting sin" is to ask yourself, "What sin am I coming the closest to committing?" Build your defenses in this area.

4. THE MIND IS A BATTLEFIELD

It's a funny thing. The devil somehow has access to our minds. He is able to conjure up thoughts there which are contrary to God's will for us. He even has access to the mind of a Christian. This whole thing can get quite confusing! Since Satan can insert thoughts in our mind, sometimes we are not sure where they are from. How are we to know if a particular thought is "my own thought" or the devil's?

All this goes on in our minds: God speaks to our minds through His Holy Spirit, we have thoughts that are our own, and the devil speaks to us — it becomes quite jumbled at times!

The point is this: if we are going to defeat Satan in our daily life, it will have to be done in our minds. The seed thoughts he plants there can take root, conceive, and finally produce sin (James 1:14-15). It is in the mind that the battle is won or lost. If he gets our minds, sooner or later he gets all of us. As a person thinks in his heart, so he becomes (Proverbs 23:7). Never get the idea you can allow your thought life to go wild without ever actually acting like you have been fantasizing. You can't! Sooner or later we all become what we think about. Fight the devil off in your mind, and you'll win the battle in your daily walk.

5. THE BIBLE IS OUR WEAPON

The best way to ensure consistent victory over temptation is a regular habit of taking in God's Word. The Bible promises this victory (Psalm 119:11). God's Word is the single best "sin preventative." This happens two ways:

a) God uses the Scripture on us. Have you ever been tempted to do something wrong when a Bible verse or person from the Bible came to mind? Why does this happen? Because the Holy Spirit brings the Bible to our memories in order to remind us an action is sinful or stupid. It's as if the Holy Spirit rapidly flips through the filing cabinet in our memories and finds the perfect scripture to help us recognize that this is sin we are being tempted to do. Has this ever happened to you? If not, could it be that the Holy Spirit finds the "Scripture" memory file almost empty in your head? He won't dictate "new Scripture" to you — that's not how it works. He merely helps you recall what you've already got in there. How's your Scripture file?

b) We use it on the devil. The second use for personal Scripture memory files is as a weapon. The one thing that will chase Satan away is God's Word — the "Sword" of the Spirit. The Bible is our only *offensive* weapon. Even Jesus, when He was tempted, repeatedly quoted the Scriptures in order to get rid of Satan (Matthew 4:4,7,10). God's Word has an authority we will never have ourselves. Have you ever tried to use logic and argument in your head against a temptation? If you have, you know that you are no match for Satan's superior debating and rationalizing skills. It is a dangerous thing to go up against the prince and power of the invisible world with nothing more than your powers of logic. You need a truly powerful weapon — God's Word! So, having a time alone with God to read and remember the Scriptures may be the single most important discipline in beating temptation.

6. THE DEVIL DOESN'T GIVE UP EASILY

Don't be surprised if after you resist the devil's temptation, quote Scripture to yourself and to him, and command him to get away from you, yet he doesn't listen! After all, tempting is his "job description." The devil is "the tempter." His business is trying to get people to disobey God. If he is especially bugging you, it may be because God has some great plans for you, and the devil suspects it. If he could get you to sin, he may be able to throw a monkey wrench into God's plans for you.

So, the devil especially focuses his attack on some people. For instance, those in full-time Christian work or in positions of leadership and influence are his favorite targets. He keeps coming back and trying to get you to fall. He may leave you "for a season"—but, watch out, he'll be back. When he tempted Jesus, he didn't give up after getting defeated over the "stones to bread" temptation. He kept coming back (Luke 4:1-13). You can expect temptation all your life. There is no level of Christian living above and beyond temptation. After you continually beat him in one area, he'll find another crack in your armor and come at you from that side. You might as well learn to beat him now, since you will be tempted throughout your whole life.[4]

7. REMEMBER, TEMPTATION IS NOT SIN

One of the tricky devices the devil uses is to try to discourage you when you are being tempted, yet haven't even given in. He puts thoughts in your mind, like, If I'm being tempted to do such an awful thing, I certainly must be an awful person. Or, Someone tempted to do that certainly could never be used by God. Wrong. Temptation is not sin — it is yielding to temptation that is sin. If the devil can't get you to give in to temptation, sometimes he will try a backup plan of getting you discouraged just because you are being tempted. Don't let this subterfuge fool you. Remember, Jesus himself was tempted — even tempted to "bow down and worship Satan." So, don't get down on yourself just because you're being tempted. Everyone is tempted. And the closer you get to the Lord, the more powerful these temptations may become.

8. FIGHT TEMPTATION — BETTER YET, FLEE IT

Sometimes, we are pretty "easy pickings" for the devil. He dangles out some morsel of sin, and we gulp it down like hungry fish. It is hardly even work for him. Just because God won't let us be tempted above what we're able to resist, doesn't mean it will be easy to resist. Resisting temptation is hard work. It's a fight. But that is what we're involved in — universal warfare against the devil, his angels, and sin. When temptation comes, fight it! Don't knuckle under without a fight. Some of us are like the quarterback who falls to his knees as soon as he sees his lineman let somebody through. Instead, run with the ball yourself! The Bible promises if we *resist* the devil, he will flee from us (James 4:7).

So, when the devil marshals his forces to try to get you to disobey God, marshal *your* forces — the name of Jesus Christ, the Word of God, your desire to obey God, the prayers of your Christian friends, and all the forces of God which are immeasurably more powerful than the devil's. If you will *resist* him, you can *beat* him!

But there is an even better strategy than fighting — fleeing. Ask yourself, What tempts me? Are there certain places where the devil is better able to tempt me? Stay away from those places. Are there certain people Satan uses to get me to do wrong things? Steer clear of those people. Are there some things which get a grip on me and entice me to do wrong — books, videos, magazines, TV shows, habits? Stay away from those things. Sometimes we fall into temptation because we hang around it too long! There is a time to stay and fight, but there is also a time to run![5]

9. YOU CAST THE DECIDING VOTE!

Really, temptation is not just between you and the devil. It is a three-way situation. God wants you to live right. The devil is hell-bound, and wants to take you with him. You cast the deciding vote. In a temptation, Jesus is on one side cheering you on, praying that you will be victorious. The devil is on the other side enticing you into rebellion against God. You are in the middle. You cast the deciding vote — either with Jesus Christ who died for you, or with the devil who intends to destroy you and drag you into hell with him forever.

The next time you are tempted, visualize yourself on the race course of a great coliseum (Hebrews 12:14). God and His angels watch from one side, the devil and his demons from the other. God and His people are encouraging you to vote with Him by staying in the race. The devil and his demons are enticing you to vote with them by giving up and dropping out. Visualize yourself surrounded by this "great cloud of witnesses." Temptation seems to be a private affair. Ultimately, it's not. Visualize this great unseen crowd around you and then make up your mind to go with God.

So, let's win it for the Lord!

Temptation can be turned into spiritual power (Luke 4:14). It's a "trick" you can use on the devil. When he tempts you to do wrong, resist him with all the determination you have. When you overcome temptation you will find a new spiritual power in your life. This is a great trick you can play on Satan. Every time he tempts you, you resist, and thus get new power. This is the ultimate trick on the devil — his temptations successfully resisted only make you stronger! He becomes a mere tool of God.

Keep hanging in there — you can beat the devil!

ENDNOTES:

1. *He knows our emotions...* Actually, temptation is not necessarily directly from the devil himself. Satan is not omnipresent and thus cannot tempt all people everywhere at one time. Apparently he has at his disposal untold numbers of demons — probably fallen angels — who carry out the tempting work at the speed of light. Some even feel each person may be assigned a personal demon or demons, sort of the equivalent of a personal guardian angel. Though we in the church often talk of "struggling with the devil" just as we refer to "sensing God talking to me," both instances may often be mediated through invisible angelic beings — God's angels and fallen angels.

2. *...the stronger we will be in the future.* This "Habit Track" is a great secret of "power living" many Christians have not discovered. A believer may lay down a "Habit track" for either good or bad. Falling into sin for a Christian often runs through these four stages: (1) The Christian faces temptation. (2) He or she struggles — not wanting to give in, yet at the same time wanting to. (3) He gives in, falling into sin. (4) The Christian feels guilty and confesses to God. What does Satan discover? A weak link, a soft spot. He will return with this temptation again. This time it is harder to resist. Let's say the Christian falls again. The devil returns again, and again, and again. What happens? Gradually the second stage disappears. The Christian quits struggling. Getting this person to sin is easy — (1) Satan delivers the temptation; (2) Christian responds with a knee-jerk sinful reaction; (3) Christian is devastated and confesses. If a Christian gets into this repeating defeated pattern of defeat he or she has laid down a stubborn "Habit Track" of disobedience. They have turned off the road at that point so often they do it almost automatically. The only way they even know they are still a Christian is that they continue to feel guilt and respond with grief and confession to God. A Christian with a sinful "Habit Track" is in a precarious position.

But there is another side to this. "Habit Track" works both ways. Using the same picture let's say that (1) Satan delivers a temptation, (2) the Christian struggles, but (3) the Christian resists and refuses to sin. What happens now? Will the devil give up? Not yet. He will return again another day and serve up that temptation again. Let's say the Christian resists again, and again, and again. What does Satan discover? A strong link, a well-defended spot. He is less and less likely to return with this temptation again. Each time he does so, it is increasingly easier for the Christian to resist. What finally happens? Gradually, the second stage disappears. The Christian quits struggling. It works this way: (1) Satan delivers the temptation; (2) Christian responds with "knee-jerk" obedience; (3) Satan is defeated and

• •

discouraged. If a Christian gets into this repeating victory pattern, he or she has laid down a stubborn "Habit Track" of obedience. They have turned toward obedience so often at this point on the road, they do it almost automatically when tempted. This is a "Habit Track" of obedience.

For more on habit track, see *Strategetics*, a tape series by the author of this book.

3. *...a weak link in your chain, a soft spot.* These weak links are not necessarily a "stronghold" of the devil. Spiritual strongholds of Satan are areas inside us under the command and control of the devil. If we are saved, we are foreign territory to the enemy. However, like the Philistines or the Trojan Horse, Satan's forces can move in and occupy territory inside us which becomes a launching place for other attacks. The "Habit Track" mentioned above relates more directly to the "spiritual stronghold" inside us. Here I am referring mostly to natural weak points which we have as a result of our genes, temperament, and our upbringing. Weak points are areas where its easier for the devil to get us to sin.

4. *...since you will be tempted through your whole life.* I do not mean here that you will experience the *same* temptations throughout your life, but that you will have *some* temptation throughout life. Satan is not so foolish as to tempt you repeatedly in an area where you have developed a "habit track." Rather he moves on to other temptations which may be more effective on you at this time. And when you have repeatedly defeated all of his temptations toward acts of sin, he switches to attitudes, holding back his biggest cannon of all for the final battle — temptation to *spiritual pride.* In this sense, a particular temptation may cease, especially after a victorious habit track is established, and you may go for years without facing that temptation. However, the devil never throws out his old "card file" on you! Sometimes after you have totally defeated him on a particular point, and years have passed without a single temptation in that area, the devil reissues an old temptation with such vengeance that it is as if you had never overcome it in the first place.

5. *There is a time to stay and fight, but there is also a time to run!* Consider the story of Joseph (Genesis 39). Here was a situation where hanging around to reason with and resist could have been deadly! Running away from some temptations — even if you leave your coat, "Mrs. Potiphar," and your dignity behind — is sometimes the best strategy to stay out of sin.

CHAPTER 11

THREE SURE-FIRE WAYS TO FALL INTO SIN

hristians sometimes fall into sin. They don't have to, but they do. I'm not an old man, but I've been around long enough to learn a little bit about why Christians do fall into sin. There are any number of ways to fall into sin, but here are three sure-fire ways to do it:

1. Hang around it

This is the easiest way to sin. Simply keep hanging around the person, place, or thing that is tempting you. One fellow who had been delivered from alcohol showed up at his pastor's home early one morning after an all-night drinking binge. The story came out in slurred speech:

> "Well, I was so happy that I felt no desire to drink that I parked my car at my old hangout to see if I still had no desire to drink. Sure enough, I didn't, so I went inside and sat down to even further test this new-found strength. I held on and still didn't want a drink. So I ordered a drink and set it on the bar in front of me. Then I crumbled. I had this overpowering urge to drink — so I did. One thing led to another, and now I am on a binge again. I guess God didn't really deliver me after all, Preacher."

How like this drunk we are. Something inside us seems to make us want to walk precariously on the edge of temptation. There are certain things — perhaps books, magazines, videos, or certain people and places — which seem to trip us up and head us in the wrong direction. Why do we keep hanging around these tempting things?

Part of the reason is that Satan has tricked us into believing we are stronger than we really are. We would rather stay near temptation and wrestle with it than to run away. Perhaps we even get a thrill out of placing our heads in the mouth of the roaring lion. We might escape unscathed. More likely, we will wind up in the belly of the tempter!

If you want to keep from falling into sin, don't hang around it. What temptation do *you* hang around?

2. Excuse it

A Christian friend of mine fell into serious immorality a number of years ago. As we counseled together, his only defense was, "I couldn't help it — it just happened."

Baloney! Sin doesn't "happen" to us as if we were innocently walking along and sin "happened" like a sudden rainstorm. Sin is a willful choice we make. We are not helpless robots and victims of our environment, desires, or glands. We are free moral agents capable of choosing what we think, say, or do. If I act unkindly, it is because I *choose* to act that way — not because I have a headache. If I think unsavory thoughts, or pass along some tidbit of gossip, it is because I *choose* to say or think those things — not because God made me a certain way or because "the devil made me do it."

If we want to overcome temptation, we must lay aside all our excuses which make sin less serious than it really is. This includes well-worn ones like, "It's such a *little* thing," "Everyone does it," "I can't help it," and "That's just the way I am." We can't get off the hook. Sin is a *personal* choice — and no excuse will cover it.

If you want to keep from falling into sin, don't excuse it. Is there some sin you are trying to excuse?

3. Struggle alone

Many of us are like the Kamikaze pilot who flew 33 missions — we make a good start but are unable to carry through. *The problem:* lack of accountability. Each of us needs another believer who will check up on our spiritual life now and then. I'm not talking about broadcasting our temptations all over the congregation. I mean asking someone to hold us accountable for our promises to God and to check up on our progress.

I adopted this practice of spiritual accountability too late in my life. Back in the 1970s I struggled with a severe temptation in desperate isolation, sharing it with nobody in fear of what they would think. Now I *know* why . . . it was pride. I was actually more concerned with what people thought of me than I was about overcoming temptation.

Later I discovered the value of an accountability relationship where someone loved me enough to hold me accountable in the areas of temptation and growth. What a difference! No longer do I struggle alone.

If you want to keep from falling into sin, get an accountability partner and quit struggling alone. Who is *your* accountability partner?

As long as Satan is prince of this earth, believers will be tempted. In fact, all he needs to do is to get you to hang around sin, excuse it, or struggle against temptation alone and he may get you.

The good news is this: we do not have to sin. Between the extreme views of the rigid Calvinists on one hand (WE ARE *NOT* ABLE *NOT* TO SIN) and a few misguided Arminians on the other (WE ARE *NOT ABLE* TO SIN) is the classic, orthodox *scriptural* view of sin in relation to the believer: WE ARE *ABLE NOT TO* SIN. And we must quickly add "by the grace of God." And *if* (not *when*) we sin, we have an Advocate with the Father! (2 John 2:1-2). That's how seriously God takes sin — and so must we. With good sense, and a lot of God's grace, we can be victorious over the many devices of the devil. It is actually possible to live obediently. It ought to be — God has commanded that you do it.

ACCOUNTABILITY

Commitments are cheap. *Keeping* commitments is expensive. How often have you made a commitment, only to forget it within a few weeks? What about that decision you made to have a Time Alone With God every day? What about your promise to witness every week? Or, how about your promise to lose 15 pounds? Do you still remember that time you made a commitment to spend more time with your kids? To date your mate? To quit wasting so much time watching TV? To make restitution for some sin in your past? To become a man or woman of prayer?

See what I mean? Commitments come easy . . . a raised hand, a short walk down the aisle, or a written promise on a card — you've made scores, perhaps hundreds in your life.

But how many have you kept? All? Most? Many? Some? Unfortunately, most Christians are lucky to have kept half their commitments. This is especially true of youth and young adults. They are quick to make commitments, but slow to keep them. This sets up a dreadful cycle of commitment, then failure, then repentance, then a repeat commitment. Have you experienced this painful cycle? Have you made a promise to God, trusting Him to change you? But within weeks, or even days, you have fallen flat on your face. Then you repent, promising the Lord you'll obey all over again.

I believe younger people tend toward this cycle more than older people. Why? Because older folk either get consistent victory or they give up. You see, if you don't get victory in this constant cycle of commitment and failure, eventually you'll simply quit making commitments. You will learn that every time you promise God something, you only fail Him. Your mind and spirit can't handle constant failure. Thus you'll simply quit trying . . . and you'll quit making commitments to God.

I've seen entire churches who had quit making commitments. They are absolutely impervious to the Holy Spirit's conviction. Powerful, specific, convicting preaching doesn't rouse them a bit from their spiritual naps. They snooze on, completely oblivious to God's spiritual alarm clock. They have programmed themselves to ignore conviction. Hearing no conviction, they won't need to make a commitment, which they have learned they cannot keep. Why is it that youth and young adults populate the altars of churches and camps? Is it because they have more sin in their lives than older people? Perhaps, but I doubt it. It is because they keep trying. Younger people keep making commitments, hoping they can keep them. Many older folk have given up.

So the question is, How can we learn to keep our commitments to God and others? When it comes to being reliable in our word, many of us do poorly with our families too. How about that job you've been promising your wife you'd do around the house? What about that promise you made to your husband to lose weight? Do you remember that trip to the amusement park you promised your kids last summer? Whatever happened to your commitment to get out of debt? How about your goal of starting a systematic savings plan? The truth is, you can't be trusted. You often are simply not a "man of your word." Your word is untrustworthy — to God or your loved ones.

Back in the early 1970s, I discovered a group of busy Christian executives who were weary of breaking promises to God and their families. They wanted to change. So they decided to get together once a month and check up on each other — to make sure they did what they said they'd do. They would list the things they intended to do during the upcoming month in their meetings. Each fellow took notes on the others' commitments. Then when they met together a month later each executive was asked how he'd done on his list. They decided to handle each man with toughness — if he hadn't kept his promises he would be rebuked as untrustworthy. And he would be put on a corrective plan by the others. These men started with simple things — like fixing a broken cabinet door in the kitchen or cleaning up the garage. It took several years of meeting together before they felt they had adequately become "men of their word." Man or woman — it is easier to make a commitment than to keep it.

These men discovered a little-known secret of commitment keeping — *accountability*. It is a most powerful secret to rescue you from the cycle of promises-broken, promises-renewed. It is the best secret to becoming a man or woman who says something and means it. It is the finest solution to a life of constant defeat and failure. It is the right step for you to take

• •

toward making commitments, then keeping them. You don't have to live with recurring procrastination. You no longer have to be satisfied with broken promises to God and others. You can start on the road to becoming a man or woman of your word — when you make a commitment, you keep it.

I believe accountability was the great secret of the early Methodist movement. John Wesley specified strict accountability in his "class meetings." Every week each member was subjected to four questions on his personal sin, temptations, victories, and struggles of the past week. The idea has come in and out of popularity down through church history. I think it's interesting that every time it falls into obscurity, holy living falters.

So what is accountability and how could you add it to your own practices of personal disciplines? I've experienced five different kinds of accountability so far. There are probably several other types of accountability. But these five have had a major impact on my commitment to live an obedient life:

A. MENTOR ACCOUNTABILITY

Mentor accountability was my first experience of someone "checking up" on me — monitoring my spiritual growth and holding me accountable for commitments. As a college freshman I met Moses Yang, an older Indonesian student who walked the holy life and loved God's Word. He took me under his wing and discipled me. We met every day, often for three to five hours, to study God's Word. He was the first person ever to be tough on me spiritually. For most of my life, if I made a commitment, I could satisfy just about everyone. Moses wasn't satisfied with commitment. He, like God, expected obedience. He would "check up on me" every day. He would ask penetrating questions about my devotions, my thoughts, my attitudes, even my dating relationships. I grew like springtime grass. Sure, I got teased for my dedication and loyalty to Moses. Other students called me a "Moses disciple" or "little Moses," but this first experience of tough accountability changed the direction of my life forever.

Mentor accountability is not usually two-way — the mentor is the "checker-upper." You place yourself under the spiritual authority of a person you trust. You spiritually submit completely to their directions regarding your spiritual growth. You agree to obediently follow their instructions. It's sort of a dangerous thing — what if they're wrong? But no accountability at all is even more dangerous. Since that year as a college freshman, I have been on the other end of mentor accountability several times — acting as the mentor. It was frightening — to have someone under my spiritual authority — someone who committed themselves to obedience to whatever I directed. I had thoughts like, "Who am I to have this authority?" I wondered, "Shouldn't they be following Jesus — not me?" I'm not completely comfortable saying with Saint Paul, "Follow me as I follow Christ." But I've done it anyway, a few times.

Becoming a parent helped. I realized that I was a spiritual mentor to my two sons. These two boys are under my spiritual authority. They will do pretty much what I say. (Well, I admit this is diminishing.) Once I realized my role in mentor accountability with my sons, it became easier to accept this role with others.

Nevertheless, I do not seek mentor accountability. It is an awesome responsibility. But periodically a desperate pastor comes to me whose life is completely tangled up. He asks for my help and guidance through the mess. When he offers himself in spiritual submission for a period of time, I usually agree. I recognize there are other valid ways to help people. But mentor accountability has been a powerful tool to help people break sinful habits, restore breaking marriages, initiate holy disciplines, and sort out tangled lives. Jesus didn't give advice, He gave commands. While I'm not Jesus, His methods of helping people who are messed up appeal to me.

B. GROUP ACCOUNTABILITY

When I was about 26 years old I experienced group accountability for the first time. Paul Swauger, Sr., (a missionary friend of mine) and I started a cell group. It was designed to have seven men who would meet once a week before breakfast. We would pray, share insights from the Word, then have an accountability time. Just the two of us met for the first few months. Then we both agreed on the third person. The three of us met for awhile until we all felt directed toward the fourth, and so on. It was a good plan and provided some great accountability in a time of my life when I needed monitoring from other men.

I think it was the fifth or sixth man who doomed the group. He was a great fellow, always encouraging everybody. Every time someone confessed shortcomings, failures, or sin he would pour soothing platitudes all over the confession. He would make some sort of a positive statement like, "No problem, all of us struggle like that." Tough accountability disappeared. Eventually the group faltered and died. I learned two lessons from this experience. Group accountability is a powerful method to help me keep commitments, and it is fragile and easily ruined.

C. DOUBLE-DATE ACCOUNTABILITY

Some of the most enjoyable accountability I've had is double-date accountability. My wife and I meet with several other couples on a monthly or quarterly basis for sharing and accountability. These double-dates are mostly fellowship times, and the accountability isn't very tough, but there is a special power in establishing accountability as a couple. This is especially true of commitments in the area of marital harmony, romance, and child rearing. These couples have changed throughout our life, though one couple has "lasted" almost twenty years. Sometimes the relationship shifts away from accountability gradually. We've noticed that the closer your association is with the other couple the harder it is to be tough on them.

Our best double-date accountability is with a couple we see only a few times a year — and both of us drive several hundred miles for an evening of spiritual accountability. Double-date accountability has its limits. But it is a great tool, especially in areas of family life accountability. It's also a good start toward this next kind of accountability.

D. SPOUSAL ACCOUNTABILITY

Talk about permanence! Spousal accountability is the longest lasting of all. If you are married, your spouse will be with you from now on. If you can get the knack of spousal accountability, you will have gained a dependable, ever present "accountant" for life. After all, who knows you best, desires your success the most, and loves you most deeply? Your life-time yokemate. But there is a knack to it. It doesn't come easily. A spouse can seem to be nagging when he/she checks up on you. And the submission you might easily grant to another accountant may come hard for you to give to your mate. And, of course, you can't expect your spouse to hold you accountable for how you treat her or him. Again, there are some things a spouse can hold you accountable for best, and others where your mate is a poor accountability partner. Nevertheless, I have had systematic mutual accountability with my wife, Sharon, for more than ten years now. It has brought us far closer together on a spiritual level than any other one Christian discipline.

E. ONE-ON-ONE ACCOUNTABILITY

I believe that one-on-one accountability is the best all-around method. Admittedly, it is the hardest to arrange and probably the most difficult to maintain. I think it is also the most effective. In one-on-one accountability two people meet regularly and check up on each other's spiritual growth. The meetings can be weekly, monthly, or, at the least, quarterly. It is a "class meeting" with only two attending.

I've had one-on-one accountability several times in my life, and each time was an apex of both spiritual growth and professional achievement. The most recent accountability contract was with a man I hold in very high esteem. It's a mutual covenant, so accountability was both ways. Sometimes such a relationship comes and goes. After several years of accountability, the sharp edge of toughness disappears. You become better friends and worse accountants. You gain a best friend, and eventually lose an accountant. I don't worry when this happens. I simply allow the friendship to develop, and look elsewhere for accountability.

I see value in all five kinds of accountability. But I honestly believe nothing will replace this hard-nosed, one-to-one accountability. If you do only one kind of accountability, I believe one-to-one is your best shot.

SO WHAT?

If you don't have a regular one-to-one accountability in your life right now, I suspect it's due to one of these three reasons: 1) You don't know *whom to ask* to be your partner; 2) You don't know *what to do* when you meet; or 3) You are guilty of *procrastination* — you just haven't got around to starting.

1. WHOM TO ASK

If you have determined you will have accountability (instead of saying, "If I find someone, I'll do this"), you'll be a long shot ahead of the game. Decide now you want to do this. Then go find the person. Once you've decided to do it, make a list of all potential accountants. List every name you can think of. Don't evaluate them, just list them. I had 14 names on such a list once. Remember, don't judge their willingness or capabilities now, just get ten or more names on your list. Once you've got your ten names set the list aside. Let it "marinate" for a few weeks. As you go about your regular routine, think over the names and see which ones the Lord seems to lead you toward. Two or three will start to surface as the best possibilities. Prayerfully consider these names until one emerges as the first choice.

Now, make an appointment to talk with your primary choice, perhaps for lunch. Take a sheet of "Accountability Questions," so you can explain what you are wanting to do. Be detailed in your description of what you are asking.

Once you've explained what you want, back off. Don't pressure. Avoid saying something like, "I've been praying about this for several weeks, and God has told me that you are the man." A partner recruited by this kind of pressure won't last. Simply explain what you are looking for and then turn your conversation to other things. Have a nice time of fellowship over the rest of your lunch.

If your first choice doesn't call in a week or two, go on down your list to other names. I expect you'll find an accountant before you've worked through five or six people, certainly before ten or fifteen.

So, now you know *whom to ask*. And you even have some ideas on how to ask them.

2. WHAT TO DO

Accountability meetings are simple. You don't need an order of worship or an agenda. You do the same things every time. Begin with your partner asking specific questions on your spiritual life. After these specific questions, move toward general accountability — questions you want asked every time. Finally, close with checking up on specific goals you've established. Then, as you gain experience together, add your own ideas. This three-point outline is not inspired, but it's a good place to begin. Later you can expand and revise your own outline as you go along. The outline:

> *1. Specific Accountability.* Several questions your accountant asks which you have listed the last time you met. If you use a checklist, he will simply ask the questions you've checked off or written in the last time you met. These are specific areas you want checked up on. They are measurable questions like, "How many days have you had Time Alone With God since we last met?" Next you give your honest report. (Obviously dishonesty is a time bomb in any accountability relationship.) If your report is one of faithfulness and progress, your partner serves up affirmation, praise, commendation, or grants you a verbal tribute, salute or applause. However if you report failure, shortfalling, and sin, he lovingly serves up a reprimand, warning, scolding, reproof, rebuke or a good old-fashioned chewing out. Not that these sessions are mostly negative — it's just that obedience is not a trivial matter.

2. *General Accountability.* Following the specific questions, move to a set of general questions you'll ask every time. John Wesley's Four Questions for class meetings are good models:

A. What known sins have you committed since we last met? If there is such, what shall we do about it?
B. What temptations have you faced?
C. How were you delivered from these temptations?
D. What have you thought, said, or done, of which you are uncertain whether it was sin or not?

3. *Goal Accountability.* Wind up by reporting on your goals. You list these the meeting before. Sometimes these are major goals which can't be accomplished in a week or month and your accountant is checking on your progress. At other times they are smaller goals which you intend to accomplish before you meet again. Here the partner may help you with a plan, or a redefinition of your goals. But still the relationship must be one of toughness.

Then you switch roles . . . now it's your turn! You go over the same outline with your partner if it's mutual accountability. That's all there is to it. Mark down next meeting's date and close with prayer.

It's not that hard, is it? Here is a clear pattern to copy. Get started and later you'll develop your own systems to meet particular needs. This outline is good enough to begin with.

3. PROCRASTINATION

Maybe you already knew whom to ask, and you knew what to do in an accountability meeting. Then why haven't you started? I suspect procrastination is the most common excuse. Your intentions are good — you plan to do it some day. Some day. You just haven't gotten around to it.

Your procrastination clearly indicates your desperate need for accountability. Procrastination is probably why you don't keep your other commitments and promises. I doubt that you've ever really intended to walk away from your promises. You just never got around to keeping them. You procrastinated. What is the remedy for procrastination? Accountability. But if you are a procrastinator, you are probably procrastinating on taking the cure. So you fully intend to have accountability, but because you don't take the next steps to begin, you are stuck in a quagmire of failure and broken promises.

Procrastinators especially need accountability. Accountability is the antidote for this disorder of your will. It may be your only hope of survival. Accountability could save you from the road "paved with good intentions." Accountability can get you beyond goal-setting to really accomplishing your goals. Accountability can take you beyond commitment to genuine spiritual life change. Accountability can guide you beyond good intentions to actually doing what you intended to do. Accountability can make you into "a man of your word."

Action breaks the bindings of procrastination. So, start now. Do something. As soon as you lay down this article. Go ahead, break the shackles of procrastination by taking action. The reason you have become such a procrastinator is your habit of reading or listening to great ideas you'd like to do, but never taking action on them. It's time to change all that. Today.

You can discover this great secret of keeping your commitments. Then you'll be able to teach others this secret. Don't let this be one more great idea you decide to do some day. Strike while the iron is hot. Take action while you are still hungering for this Christian discipline.

Is there any good reason why you shouldn't start making your list of prospective accountability partners right now?

CHAPTER 13

How To Have A Day Alone With God

A daily time alone with God or daily devotions has always come hard for me. I don't mean that I ignore this spiritual discipline — it's just that a bit of time each morning is not good enough for me.

Where I Was

It takes me a full half hour just to quiet down enough to really get serious with God. I knew I needed to spend more time with Him, and my morning devotions were sort of like an "invocation" — a nice thing to do each morning, but not really enough of a serious effort at spirituality.

What I Tried First

I struggled with this problem for several years, finally concluding that what I needed to do was spend more time each day. I figured I could get up at 5:00 a.m. or so and spend a full hour or two with the Lord each day. Now, this is a good idea, and it works admirably for some, but it didn't work for me. The problem was my schedule — most of the time it is so messed up that a regular time was impossible. Half of the time my schedule was under the control of other people — hosts, ministerials, conventions, camps, and conferences. Though it works for many people, the "early to rise" solution didn't work for me. Yet I was still gravely dissatisfied with the time I set apart for pure devotion to God.

What Changed It All

Then a new thought struck. *What if this were my wife I was trying to*

• •

develop a deeper relationship with? I've never come home from a confer-
ence and sat down with my wife to say, "I'm not satisfied with the depth
of our relationship. Let's get up at 5:00 a.m. each morning and talk with
each other." (We have a pretty good marriage, but I'm not sure it could
sustain this!) Sure, I daily and systematically express my love and devotion to Sharon through little actions and words. We even set apart a
"debriefing" time each day to catch up on each other's lives.

But I realized the thing that really made the priority statement to her
was our "family days." In my thirties I began the practice of writing a big,
large "F" on several days each month, designating them as "family days."
These days were set aside to sneak away with Sharon, go on a walk, laze
around and share deeply with each other, and to spend the evening with
the kids. They weren't highly organized or scheduled days, just days with
which I would allow nothing to interfere. During these days we spend
large amounts of time just sharing together about our developing lives and
relationships with each other, the children, the church, and God.

The parallel to my spiritual life was stunning to me. My daily time
alone with God was important, to be sure. But what was lacking in my
relationship with the Lord were large blocks of time dedicated exclusively
to the development of our relationship.

Then I remembered an idea a friend of mine had shared a year or so
earlier. Dwight Robertson, a successful youth pastor, told how he
scheduled "blackout days." He shared how he took a black marker pen
and literally blacked out an entire day from his calendar making it
impossible to schedule anything else that day. He had dedicated these
days to developing his relationship with the Lord. The seed of this idea,
which had been sitting back there for a year now began to sprout. I
decided I needed a whole day to spend alone with God for the sake of
our developing relationship.

The Solution

When I first began this discipline, I would set apart this day "as I needed it." When things got particularly frustrating, when I sensed my spiritual
batteries were drained low, or when I faced an upcoming major spiritual
challenge, I would slip away for a day alone with God. These days had
such an influence on my life that I finally began scheduling them on a
monthly basis. Here are some of the things I have learned about establishing the discipline of a periodic DAWG - "Day Alone With God."

Where To Go

When the weather is good, I like to go outside for my Day Alone With God. When I first began, I still had children around the house all day. I would often go to a state park about fifteen miles from my home where I spent the day in the wooded area beside a large lake. I can't sit very long for anything, so being out of doors gave me an opportunity to get up and "walk and pray" when I got tired of sitting. Since I often take my DAWG during the week, a city park was my backup plan. There's a softball field which is completely abandoned through the week, and I would sometimes spend my day alone with God just outside the right field fence.

In the winter time, it was harder. There was a retreat center just an hour from my home which I used some during cold days. I have a friend in Michigan who uses the Primary age Sunday school classroom. (He says no one ever goes in a Primary Sunday school classroom during the week!) A pastor friend of mine spends his Day Alone With God in a parishioner's summer cottage which is graciously provided for him. I know one mother of a preschooler who drops her child off at a baby-sitter and takes off a half day at her own home each month for this discipline. I met a man in Pennsylvania who actually constructed a "prophet's chamber" up in the woods behind his house where he could spend his Day Alone With God. Seeing that "prophet's chamber" gave me a hidden dream — to have one for myself. After more than a decade of moving from place to place for my DAWG my dream was fulfilled. A boy we taught in our midweek CYC group years ago grew up to be a contractor and offered to build a farmhouse for us on our country land near Indianapolis. I shared my dream for some sort of attic hideaway for a DAWG and his face lit up. "I'll build it for you! Leave it up to me." He did, and I now have my own little heated hideaway tucked away in our attic. To have a reliable *place* makes this discipline much easier.

Let your imagination fly and think of the kind of place you could spend your DAWG. Before I had my "upper room" I even spent some entire days in my automobile. There is a certain seclusion, privacy, and intimacy in an automobile that's hard to find elsewhere. Maybe that sounds weird to you, but the question is, where could *you* go for a DAWG?

What To Take

1. *Bible* - Obviously, if you take only *one* thing, this is it.
2. *Colored pencils/pens* - I have found the absolute best time to do Bible marking is on a DAWG.

3. *Note pad or paper* - To jot down your insights.
4. *Concordance* - I usually forget this, but I generally regret not having it.
5. *Lawn chair* - If you're going to be outside.
6. *Tape player* - Occasionally edifying and worshipful music sets the mood for my DAWG.
7. *A book or two* - But be careful not to make the whole day a book-reading day.
8. *Sweater or jacket* - If you are an active person, sitting around most of the day usually gives you a chill.
9. *Spiritual life notebook* - To note insights and prayer records.

One thing you do *not* want to take is paperwork. If you're like me, you will almost always choose spiritual work over spiritual devotion. I love to produce, produce, produce. I generally measure the success of my day with "how much I got done." That's why I have to wrestle so much to get myself to do spiritual and devotional things. So I have to leave my work at the office or I find myself gravitating to my "to do" list and away from relationship development with the Lord.

There are only two exceptions I allow to this. First, I take a note pad, and when I think of something I need to do, I write it down and get it out of my mind. Second, if I am developing a vision for my ministry or planning my year's activity, I do this on my DAWG. I want these sorts of things to *grow out of* a time of devotion.

One other thing I often do *not* take is any sort of watch or clock. I am such a time-conscious person that I keep checking up to see "how I'm doing" throughout the day. It's better for me if I simply give the whole day to the Lord until dark.

What To Do

1. *Read the Bible.* This is the perfect time to read great blocks of Scripture. Most of our Bible reading is in short spurts. We don't read anything else that way — just the Bible. A DAWG gives us the chance to read entire books of the Bible, which is how they were meant to be read. Usually you can read a book through several times in one day, allowing its message and truth to saturate you in a way that "snippet reading" never will. I always read with a pencil in hand so I can scribble all over the margins. If my mind begins to wander or clog up, I read aloud. This usually refocuses my thoughts on the scripture in front of me. Once in a while, a topical study is fun to do. But I have to be careful not to use this

time to prepare Sunday school lessons or a message. It is for me and God.

2. *Fast.* Sometimes fasting will focus your spiritual energies more intensely. But if "visions of sandwiches dance in your head," fasting could actually divert your interest away from relationship development with the Lord. You must do what is best for you.

3. *Pray.* Obviously the whole day is set aside to develop your relationship with the Lord. That means reading His Word, talking to Him, and listening to Him. I intersperse my Scripture reading with prayer. When my mind begins to "burn out" on Scripture reading, I spend a chunk of time chatting with the Lord. This is not a time for formal, fancy, cathedral-type praying. It is a time to be honest, frank, and simple in communication with God. It is a time for open confession, worshipful adoration, grateful thanksgiving, bold requests, and committed surrender.

When it's just you and God, the pauses in your prayer don't really matter. A DAWG is a perfect time to develop an extensive prayer list and pray through it. Unless you are a professional monk, you probably can't daily pray through all of the requests you have thought of. But a periodic DAWG allows for a more systematic approach to a longer list of prayer requests.

4. *Write.* I don't know if you're like me, but I can't do anything without eventually writing something down. And I have found that unless I write it down, it is somehow incomplete. If you have fallen behind on your spiritual life journal, your DAWG is a perfect time to catch up.

Even if you never keep a journal, try keeping one only on your Days Alone With God over the next few years. Write down what's happening in your spiritual life. Write down your reflections on trials you are going through. Write down the temptations you are now facing and how you plan to overcome them. Write down people who have had major influence in your life. Make a list of the people whom you are probably influencing in their spiritual lives. Write out your personal commitments to the Lord between this day and your next DAWG. Write a letter to your spouse or someone else, sharing important matters with them. Write an evangelistic letter to some unsaved person. Write down scriptural truths which jumped out at you today. The chances are you'll remember most of what you have written down.

5. *Memorize Scripture.* Most of us fail miserably at this spiritual discipline. Part of the reason is we try to cram it in along with everything else we're doing in our busy schedules. Setting aside an entire DAWG allows you to add a new scripture to your stock. It is completely feasible to memorize ten verses on one of these days, and remember them the rest of your life.

6. *Meditate.* I use this word in both of its meanings. First, meditate on

Scripture — that is, turn it over and over again in your mind, thinking on it, much like a cow chews its cud. Second, meditate in the sense of just plain relaxing/resting/thinking about nothing. If you are really exhausted, you might even doze off for awhile. Don't worry about this "conking out"; just fall asleep with God's thoughts on your mind, and wake up the same way. During these times of quiet listening, God often reveals His will to me. Perhaps you are a better listener asleep than when you are awake! In any case, *be yourself.*

A DAWG can be a spiritual dynamo in your life. In the hectic rushed schedule of "doing God's work," it is so easy to allow our spiritual energy to drain out. An entire day blocked out each month to develop that close relationship with God, recharging your spiritual batteries, is a great secret to keeping your spiritual edge. My only regret is that I did not discover this secret much sooner in my Christian walk.

What about you? Does taking an entire day off for "devotions" seem extreme? Or would you like to try this a few times? If you did, where could you go? When could you have your first day? Maybe even a half-day? If you don't start now, at about what age would you like to try this discipline?

BECOMING A "MORNING PERSON"

My wife Sharon is a morning person. She cheerfully pops out of bed every day, warm blood coursing through her veins, a song in her heart, and thoughts of projects to start, devotions to begin, and work to get done.

Not me! I start in low gear. To tease me about my morning laziness, she once got a button announcing "SOMETIMES I WAKE UP GROUCHY." Underneath were the tiny words "AND SOMETIMES I LET HIM SLEEP."

I've always been a night owl. Morning people sing in the shower . . . even before breakfast! I started each day with several refrains of the snooze button. Eventually I'd grumpily stumble out of bed, stagger to the living room and collapse on the couch for a few more precious minutes of sleep.

Morning people disgusted me . . . especially their nauseating cheerfulness in the most gloomy part of the day. Cheerfulness seemed inappropriate in the morning — like laughter at a funeral. Cheerful morning people seemed sick.

Worse yet, morning people have this air of superiority . . . as if night owls are inferior and undisciplined. You know, "Hi Ho, Hi Ho, it's off to devotions we go." Their favorite verse is "Early will I seek Him," and they like to tell night owls how they always "start off the day right" with the Lord. Night owls are lucky to get through a blurry devotional time without falling back to sleep.

All this makes the night owl life rather miserable. Does anybody ever drive by a pastor's home at 2:00 a.m. and remark "Now there's a disciplined preacher — probably reading his Bible." No. At 2:00 a.m. they figure you're watching the late show. But if they come by at 5:30 a.m.

117

and see the lights on, they say, "Saw the preacher up early this morning — boy, he's sure a hard worker!" Unfair! I actually heard of one night owl pastor who rigged up a timer so the lights in his study would go on early, just to impress his farming community!

I always felt my genes got crossed up. I figured I was born this way. Writers are infamous for being night owls, so I accepted it as "just me." Then I got to know a famous author I really respected. He was a night owl who said he'd become a morning person. I wondered, "Could *I* become a morning person?"

It can be done! Since then I *have* actually become a morning person. It did not come easily or quickly. The process took several years. But I can testify that it is possible for night owls to become morning persons — if you really want to. Do you hate mornings, and really want to change? Here's how:

1. Determine if God wants you to do this.

If you want to become a morning person merely to be considered more disciplined and improve your image, you probably won't make it. Or if morning people have imposed guilt on you so much that you're ready to buckle in, that is probably not enough motivation. Doing this for personal professional reasons may not be enough to get you changed. You need God's help. Changing with God's help is hard enough. Without His help, change comes harder, maybe even not at all.

However, if you sense a spiritual conviction about the whole thing, your chance of actually changing multiplies. Do you believe God wants you to change? That's the *first* question!

2. Examine the roots of your present habits.

People are probably not born night owls or morning persons. Somewhere along the line you developed the entrenched habits of a night owl. Anyway an inclination does not determine a destiny. You had to "get into the habit" of acting on your inclination to form a life pattern.

When did your owlish habit start? Recall your childhood bedtime habits. How about high school? College? Scrutinize how you've reinforced the night owl habit through the years. Even if you believe your owlishness was a birth trait, confess the habit as an adopted one. In other words, as long as you claim, "I was just born this way," you'll never change. But once you agree that you don't *have* to act on any sort of inclination you were born with, then you have moved one giant step toward being changed.

3. Pick a bed time and stick to it. I don't need discipline in getting up — it is in going to bed that I need discipline. I have always hated to end the day. I'm always wanting to complete one more letter, jot down one more idea, write one more chapter, watch one more TV show, have one more . . . This lack of discipline at night was half my problem. Once I learned to stick to a bedtime hour, even if I didn't fall asleep right away, getting up in the morning became possible.

4. Set a rising time and stick to it. Pick a sensible time to get up and stick to it — every day. Totally abandon "sleeping in" even on your day off. Set your alarm permanently for your rising time and place the alarm out of reach so you can't use the snooze button. If you absolutely must "catch up" on your sleep (most sleep experts say you can't), do it in the afternoons — but for six months straight never sleep in during the morning hours. *Never.* Sleeping in is the equivalent of an alcoholic going on a "binge." All of last week's gains can be lost in one morning.

However, be realistic in setting your rising time. Many of my own attempts to change failed because of unrealistic expectations. I'd hear about Martin Luther or John Wesley and feel condemned about my morning laziness. If John Wesley could get up at 4:00 a.m., I should do it too. So I'd set my alarm for 4:00 a.m. with great plans to start the day with several hours of powerful prayer. Too much change too quickly. In a week or two my plans had fizzled. It is much better to start with a realistic time and stick to it. After a year or so at that time, you can then shave off a half hour of sleep the next year. The point here is to set a sensible goal, then stick with it until it becomes habitual.

5. Don't expect to feel like a morning person. C'mon. You remember what we say to new Christians about feelings. Apply that thinking here. If you go on feelings, you'll give up quickly. Feeling like a morning person — literally *feeling* cheery and motivated when you get up — is the result of years of habit. Start with *behavior* — get up early. As you repeat the behavior it will eventually become a *habit.* When the habit is ingrained you will actually become a morning person. Finally, *after the habit is "second nature" the feelings* will come . . . only then do you actually experience morning person sensations. For now, forget feelings — work on the habit.

6. Quit telling yourself you're not a morning person. One of the reasons you are not a morning person is that you have told yourself that so long. Your attitude toward mornings is a result of years of "self-hypnosis" — repeatedly telling yourself and others, "I'm not a morning person." You've said it so often that you automatically act like it. Hating mornings is now so much a part of your self-identity you can be nothing but a morning-hater. Being a night owl is part of your very "persona." You hear a prerecorded message every morning.

To change this you must record a new message in the morning section of your psyche. You must reprogram your mind. You do that through self-affirmation — what you repeatedly say to yourself and others.

Begin telling yourself, "I'm becoming a morning person." Announce it to others too. As you start your new behaviors, and they become habits, change your self-affirmation to "I *am* a morning person." Watch this simple self-talk begin to change your attitude toward mornings. I felt silly doing this at first. I'd stagger out of bed and mumble sarcastically, "I'm a morning person." I even put a little card on my dresser for a while: "Good morning, morning person." But silly as that act was, I was indeed becoming just that. Eventually I was able to reprogram my attitude toward mornings. As long as you keep telling yourself you are what you are, you'll never become anything more.

7. Consider timing in all of this. If you really want to become a morning person, pick a good time to begin. Since becoming a morning person is essentially a habit, laying down a new rut takes time and persistence. Don't start during Christmas vacation, or the week you are leading an "overnighter" with the youth group or serving as a counselor at youth camp. Pick a six-week period when you can stick consistently with your new habits every day.

Most habits take a minimum of six weeks to get started, plus another five months to develop as a lifetime permanent change. In any change of behavior or attitude, most defeats occur during the first six weeks. Pick the right period of time to start.

8. Getting older will help. In my thirties I got a chance to do a traveling tour with several friends including Lee Haines and David Keith. Both of these men seemed to be in a contest to prove who could get up earliest. I had traveled with David Keith for years and was always shocked by his refusal to set an alarm clock — even if we were leaving at 4:00 a.m. "Oh, I'll be awake," he would insist. Impossible! But he would be. Lee Haines was just as bad. He was one of those types who got up and walked a couple miles at dawn or before. Both men even ate breakfast. How disgusting to me at the time — they actually put food in

• •

their stomachs before noon! As they rattled about in the room in the pre-dawn hours, I would groan, then roll over for a few more hours' sleep and a more decent rising hour.

I talked to Lee Haines once about my morning groaning period. He promised that as I got older, waking up would get easier. Most older people agree with this. So, if you are young, and want to become a morning person — you could simply wait until you reach your fifties and your problem may solve itself!

I couldn't wait. I decided to become a morning person before it happened naturally. So I followed the above regimen. I can honestly now say, "I'm a morning person." I too can now savor the sweet sensations morning people have when they have finished several important tasks while their neighbors are still asleep. Now I too can bask in the feelings of spiritual success in morning prayers before many folk have even awakened.

Admittedly, this teaching isn't for everyone. If you are a morning person, all this seems so elementary. For others, the idea is totally unattractive. I taught college students several years. To them, this idea was about as alluring as a chapter on "How to enjoy eating dead cats." Most collegians can't imagine why an individual might even *want* to be a morning person.

But many adults are stuck back in their collegian era. I was for years. Then I decided I could change, with God's help. Do you want to change? You can if you really want to. Especially if you think God wants you to change. However, if you really believe that "this is just the way I am," you think there's nothing wrong with it, and you have no *desire* to change . . . well, then you are stuck with being what you are.

Perhaps you are wondering why I would waste the final chapter of this book on becoming a morning person.

I didn't. This chapter and this book are about *change* . . . any positive change. Forget becoming a morning person for the moment. This chapter is symbolic in a way. Certainly if a night owl like me can become a morning person there are other, far more important changes I can and should experience. And what about you? What change do *you* need? Are you saying, "This is just who I am" about something in your life? Are *you* saying, "I was born with this"? Is God talking to you about changing some pattern, habit, desire, or thought pattern in your life?

Where do *you* need to change? How will God help you *do it*?

The principles about changing are the same — whether it's in becoming a "morning person" or in resisting materialism, sexual sin, or in starting habits like a Day Alone With God, or an accountability relationship.

These universal "change principles" which we have applied to changing into a morning person adapt to all change:

1. Make it a spiritual issue.
2. Examine the roots of your problem.
3. Start with a "root discipline."
4. Establish a habit.
5. Don't expect feelings at first.
6. Use positive self-talk.
7. Time your start-up carefully.
8. Spiritual maturity will help.

If you are saying, "I don't feel like God wants me to become a morning person," then the question to you is, "Then what is God talking to you about changing?" Apply these change principles to the area God is putting His finger on now. You *can* change. Really, you can!

APPENDIX

ACCOUNTABILITY QUESTIONS

Select the questions you want your accountability partner to ask you about in the next meeting.

I. 75 Specific Accountability Questions:

_____ 1. Have you had daily Time Alone With God since we last met?

_____ 2. How many Days Alone With God have you taken?

_____ 3. Have your thoughts been pure and free from lust?

_____ 4. Have you dated your spouse every week?

_____ 5. Have you taken a day off each week?

_____ 6. Have you had a daily debriefing time with your spouse?

_____ 7. Is there anyone against whom you are holding a grudge?

_____ 8. Is there any emotional attachment with someone of the opposite sex which could develop dangerously?

_____ 9. With whom could such an attachment develop in the future?

_____ 10. Have you given unselfishly to your mate's needs?

_____ 11. Are there any unresolved conflicts with your mate?

_____ 12. Have you been harsh or unkind in the use of your tongue?

_____ 13. How often have you had family altar since we last met?

_____ 14. How often have you shared your faith? When? What happened?

_____ 15. How much time have you spent with your children? Doing what?

_____ 16. Have you spread falsehoods about another — slander?

_____ 17. Have you spread hurtful truth about another — gossip?

_____ 18. Do you have any unmade restitutions?

_____ 19. Are you discipling your child? Mate? How? When?

_____ 20. Is your practice of journaling up to date?

_____ 21. How much have you fasted since we last met?

_____ 22. Have you had nightly prayers with your spouse?

_____ 23. Report on your memorizing and meditating on Scripture.

_____ 24. How are you improving in your relationship with your mate?

_____ 25. Is there a brother you should try to restore from sin?

_____ 26. When did you last give a thoughtful gift to your mate?

_____ 27. In what ways have you been tempted to be proud?

_____ 28. How have you given to the needy since we last met?

_____ 29. How much time have you wasted watching TV?

_____ 30. What about questionable movies, magazines, or videos?

_____ 31. Are you completely out of installment debt?

_____ 32. How are you avoiding materialism?

_____ 33. Have you exaggerated or lied since we last met?

_____ 34. Have you been able to ignore carnal, complaining, petty people?

_____ 35. What spiritual growth books have you read since we met?

_____ 36. Of what are you afraid? How will you defy this fear?

_____ 37. How have you played "Team Ball" with others since we last met?

_____ 38. Have you had a critical spirit since we last met?

_____ 39. In what special ways have you shown love to your mate?

_____ 40. Have you been fully submissive to authority?

_____ 41. Who is it that you are tempted to envy, or be jealous of?

_____ 42. Is there any believer with whom you are out of harmony?

_____ 43. Whom are you discipling and mentoring? How?

_____ 44. Was there a time when your love for God was hotter?

_____ 45. How have you attempted to make peace between others?

_____ 46. Have you taken anything not belonging to you, large or small?

_____ 47. What sexual sin have you been most tempted to commit?

_____ 48. Have you a practice which may be a stumbling block to others?

_____ 49. Have you avoided outbursts of anger or rage?

_____ 50. About what have you been inclined to boast?

_____ 51. Have you been tempted to give up? How? Why?

_____ 52. How have you clarified your life's mission since we last met?

_____ 53. Have you avoided fighting, quarreling, dissension, and factions?

_____ 54. How have you shown enduring patience since we last met?

_____ 55. Have you avoided obscenity, foolish talk, and coarse jokes?

_____ 56. In what ways have you been tempted to greed?

_____ 57. Have you selfish ambition? How pure is your desire to achieve?

_____ 58. Is there hate, malice, or ill will in your heart for anyone?

_____ 59. Is there any sin, inward or outward, which has dominion over you so that you are habitually falling in this area?

_____ 60. How have you expressed thanksgiving to God and others?

_____ 61. How have you shown submission and respect to your husband?

_____ 62. How have you shown love and tenderness to your wife?

_____ 63. Have you frivolously wasted words since we last met?

_____ 64. Have you participated in fruitless arguments?

_____ 65. Do you have a teachable spirit?

_____ 66. Have you shown favoritism toward the rich or powerful? How?

_____ 67. In what way have you launched out in faith since we last met?

_____ 68. Have you abused your power over others? How?

_____ 69. Have you deceitfully manipulated people for your own benefit?

_____ 70. Have you been guilty of worry, anxiety, or distrust of God?

_____ 71. In what ways have you shown brotherly kindness?

_____ 72. Is there any sin of another which you have come to tolerate?

_____ 73. How have you sought opportunities to serve, listen, and help?

_____ 74. How have you cared for the needy since we last met?

_____ 75. To whom did you show Christ's love since we last met? How?

II. John Wesley's "Four Questions" for weekly class meetings:

_____ A. What known sins have you committed since we last ?
If there is such, what shall we do about it?

_____ B. What temptations have you faced?

_____ C. How were you delivered from these temptations?

_____ D. What have you thought, said or done, of which you are
uncertain whether it was sin or not?

III. GOALS — To be held accountable for:

1.

2.

3.

4.

5.